797,885 Books
are available to read at

www.ForgottenBooks.com

Forgotten Books' App
Available for mobile, tablet & eReader

ISBN 978-1-334-39691-5
PIBN 10722144

This book is a reproduction of an important historical work. Forgotten Books uses state-of-the-art technology to digitally reconstruct the work, preserving the original format whilst repairing imperfections present in the aged copy. In rare cases, an imperfection in the original, such as a blemish or missing page, may be replicated in our edition. We do, however, repair the vast majority of imperfections successfully; any imperfections that remain are intentionally left to preserve the state of such historical works.

Forgotten Books is a registered trademark of FB &c Ltd.
Copyright © 2017 FB &c Ltd.
FB &c Ltd, Dalton House, 60 Windsor Avenue, London, SW19 2RR.
Company number 08720141. Registered in England and Wales.

For support please visit www.forgottenbooks.com

1 MONTH OF FREE READING

at

www.ForgottenBooks.com

By purchasing this book you are eligible for one month membership to ForgottenBooks.com, giving you unlimited access to our entire collection of over 700,000 titles via our web site and mobile apps.

To claim your free month visit:
www.forgottenbooks.com/free722144

* Offer is valid for 45 days from date of purchase. Terms and conditions apply.

English
Français
Deutsche
Italiano
Español
Português

www.forgottenbooks.com

Mythology Photography **Fiction**
Fishing Christianity **Art** Cooking
Essays Buddhism Freemasonry
Medicine **Biology** Music **Ancient Egypt** Evolution Carpentry Physics
Dance Geology **Mathematics** Fitness
Shakespeare **Folklore** Yoga Marketing
Confidence Immortality Biographies
Poetry **Psychology** Witchcraft
Electronics Chemistry History **Law**
Accounting **Philosophy** Anthropology
Alchemy Drama Quantum Mechanics
Atheism Sexual Health **Ancient History**
Entrepreneurship Languages Sport
Paleontology Needlework Islam
Metaphysics Investment Archaeology
Parenting Statistics Criminology
Motivational

DICKS' STANDARD PLAYS.

THE SHAUGHRAUN.

BY DION BOUCICAULT, ESQ.

ORIGINAL COMPLETE EDITION.—PRICE ONE PENNY.

⁂ This Play can be Performed without Risk of Infringing any Rights.

LONDON: JOHN DICKS, 313, STRAND.

DICKS' STANDARD PLAYS
AND
FREE ACTING DRAMA.
FOR THE REPRESENTATION OF WHICH THERE IS NO LEGAL CHARGE.

1 Othello
2 School for Scandal
3 Werner
4 She Stoops to Conquer
5 The Gamester
6 King Lear
7 New way to Pay old Debts
8 Road to Ruin
9 Merry wives of Windsor
10 The Iron Chest
11 Hamlet
12 The Stranger
13 Merchant of Venice
14 The Honeymoon
15 Pizarro
16 Man of the World
17 Much Ado about Nothing
18 The Rivals
19 Damon and Pythias
20 Macbeth
21 John Bull
22 Fazio
23 Speed the Plough
24 Jane Shore
25 Evadne
26 Antony and Cleopatra
27 The Wonder
28 The miller and his men
29 The Jealous Wife
30 Therese
31 Brutus
32 The Maid of Honour
33 A Winter's Tale
34 The Poor Gentleman
35 The Castle Spectre
36 The Heir-at-Law
37 Love in a Village
38 A Tale of mystery
39 Douglas
40 The Critic
41 George Barnwell
42 Grecian Daughter
43 As You Like It
44 Cato
45 The Beggars' Opera
46 Isabella
47 The Revenge
48 Lord of the Manor
49 Romeo and Juliet
50 Sardanapalus
51 The Hypocrite
52 Venice Preserved
53 The Provoked Husband
54 Clandestine marriage
55 Fair Penitent
56 Two Gentlemen of Verona
57 Fatal Curiosity
58 Belle's Stratagem
59 Manfred
60 Rule a Wife, &c.
61 Bertram
62 Wheel of Fortune
63 The Duke of Milan
64 Good-Natured Man
65 King John
66 Beaux' Stratagem
67 Arden of Faversham
68 Trip to Scarborough
69 Lady Jane Grey
70 Rob Roy
71 Roman Father
72 The Provoked wife
The Two Foscari
Foundling of the Forest
 All the World's a Stage
 Richard III
 Bold Stroke for a wife
 Castle of Sorrento
 The Inconstant

87 Cymbeline
88 She Would, &c:
89 Deserted Daughter
90 Wives as They Were, and maids as They Are
91 Every man in his humour
92 Midsummer Night's Dream
93 Tamerlane
94 Bold Stroke for a husband
95 Julius Cæsar
96 All for Love
97 The Tempest
98 Richard Cœur de Lion
99 The Mourning Bride
100 The bashful man
101 Barbarossa
102 The Curfew
103 Merchant of Bruges
104 Giovanni in London
105 Timon of Athens
106 Honest Thieves
107 West Indian
108 The Earl of Essex
109 The Irish Widow
110 The Farmer's Wife
111 Tancred and Sigismunda
112 The Panel
113 Deformed Transformed
114 The Soldier's Daughter
115 Monsieur Tonson
116 The Black Prince
117 School for Wives
118 Coriolanus
119 The Citizen
120 The First Floor
121 The Foundling
122 Oroonoko
123 Love a-la-Mode
124 Richard II
125 Siege of Belgrade
126 Samson Agonistes
127 Maid of the mill
128 One o'Clock
129 Who's the Dupe?
130 Mahomet
131 Duplicity
132 The Devil to Pay
133 Troilus
134 War
162 Suspicious Husband
163 Dog of Montargis
164 The Heiress

172 The Chances
173 Follies of a Day
174 Titus Andronicus
175 Paul and Virginia
176 Know your own mind
177 The Padlock
178 Constant Couple
179 Better Late than Never
180 My Spouse and I
181 Every One has his Fault
182 The Deuce is in him
183 Adopted Child
184 Lovers' Vows
185 Maid of the Oaks
186 The Duenna
187 Turnpike Gate
188 Lady of Lyons
189 Miss in her Teens
190 Twelfth Night
191 Lodoiska
192 Earl of Warwick
193 Fortune's Frolics
194 Way to keep him
195 Braganza
196 No Song no Supper
197 Taming of the Shrew
198 Spanish Student
199 Double Dealer
200 Mock Doctor
201 Fashionable lover
202 The Guardian
203 Cain
204 Rosina
205 Love's Labour Lost
206 The Hunchback
207 The Apprentice
208 Raising the Wind
211 April Day
213 Pericles
214 Robinson Crusoe
215 He's much to Blame
216 Ella Rosenberg
217 The Quaker
218 School of Reform
246 Virginius
247 School for Arrogance
248 The Two Gregories

256 Dominique
257 Chapter of Accidents
258 Descarte
259 Hero and Leander
260 Cure for Heartache
261 Siege of Damascus
262 The Secret
263 Deaf and Dumb
264 Banks of the Hudson
265 The Wedding Day
266 Laugh when you can
267 What Next?
268 Raymond and Agnes
269 Lionel and Clarissa
270 Red crow
271 The Contrivance
272 Broken Sword
273 Polly Honeycomb
274 Nell Gwynne
275 Cymon
276 Perfection
277 Count of Narbonne
278 Of Age To-morrow
279 Orphan of China
280 Pedlar's Acre
281 Mogul's Tale
282 Othello Travestie
283 Law of Lombardy
284 Day after the wedding
285 The Jew
286 Irish Tutor
287 Such Things Are
288 The Wife
289 Dragon of Wantley
290 Sail Dhuv
291 Lying Valet
292 Lily of St. Leonards
293 Oliver Twist
294 The Housekeeper
295 Child of Nature
296 Home, Sweet Home
297 Which is the man?
298 Caius Gracchus
299 Mayor of Garratt
300 Woodman
301 Midnight Hour
302 Woman's Wit
303 The Purse
304 Votary of Wealth
305 Life Buoy
306 Wild Oats
307 Rookwood
308 Gambler's Fate
309 Herne the Hunter
310 "Yes!" and "No!"
311 The Sea-captain
312 Eugene Aram
313 Wrecker's Daughter
314 Alfred the Great
315 { Virginia mummy
     { Intrigue
316 { My Neighbour's wife
     { Married Bachelor
317 Richelieu
318 Money
319 Ion
320 The Bridal
321 Paul Pry
322 Love-chase
323 Glencoe
324 { Spitalfields weaver
     { Stage Struck
325 Robert Macaire
326 Country Squire
327 Athenian Captive
328 { Barney the Baron
     { Happy man
329 Der Freischutz
330 Hush money

THE SHAUGHRAUN.
AN ORIGINAL DRAMA, IN THREE ACTS,
ILLUSTRATIVE OF IRISH LIFE AND CHARACTER.
BY DION BOUCICAULT, ESQ.

[See page 19.

Dramatis Personæ.
First Performed at Wallack's Theatre, New York, 1875.

CAPTAIN MOLINEUX (a young English Officer, commanding a detachment at Ballyragget) ... Mr. H. J. Montague.
ROBERT FFOLLIOTT (a young Irish Gentleman—under sentence as a Fenian—in love with Arte O'Neale) ... ... Mr. C. A. Stevenson.
FATHER DOLAN (the Parish Priest of Suil-a-beg, his tutor and guardian) ... ... Mr. John Gilbert.
CORRY KINCHELA (a Squireen) Mr. Edward Arnott.
HARVEY DUFF (a Police Agent in disguise of a peasant, under the name of Keach), Mr. Harry Beckett.
CONN (the Shaughraun, the soul of every fair, the life of every funeral, the first fiddle at all weddings and patterns ... ... Mr. Dion Boucicault.
SERGEANT JONES (of the 41st), Mr. W. J. Leonard.

SULLIVAN ⎫
REILLY   ⎪
MANGAN   ⎬ Peasants ⎫ Mr. Edwin.
DOYLE   ⎪   ⎬
DONOVAN ⎭   ⎭
ARTE O'NEAL (in love with Robert), Miss Jeffries Lewis.
CLAIRE FFOLLIOTT (a Sligo Lady), Miss Ada Dyas.
MRS. O'KELLY (Conn's Mother), Madame Ponisi.
MOYA (Father Dolan's Niece, in love with Conn), Mrs. Jane Burke.
BRIDGET MADIGAN (a Keener)... ... Mrs. Sefton.
NANCY MALONE (a Keener) ... ...
Peasants, Soldiers, Constabulary.

No. 390. Dicks' Standard Plays.

COSTUME.

CAPTAIN MOLINEUX.—Full suit of regimentals—infantry officer's tunic—crimson sash—shako and sword.

ROBERT FFOLLIOTT.—Dark blue pilot coat and trousers—black glazed sailor's hat—long gray ulster.

FATHER DOLAN.—Plain black clerical frock (no collar)—black knee breeches and gaiters—cassock—broad-brimmed hat, and cane.

CORRY KINCHELA.—*1st Dress*: Green cut-away coat—light breeches and waistcoat—Napoleon boots. *2nd Dress*: Scarlet hunting-coat—white waistcoat and breeches, and top-boots—white hat, and hunting-whip. *3rd Dress*: Frieze overcoat, and broad-brimmed wide-awake hat.

HARVEY DUFF.—Ragged gray frieze overcoat—Irish billycock hat—red waistcoat—brown cord breeches—patched gray stockings—ankle-jacks—no neckerchief—check shirt-collar, open, and throat visible.

CONN.—*1st Dress*: Old patched scarlet hunting-coat—brown cord breeches—old yellow top boots—check shirt, and old black velvet hunting-cap. *2nd Dress*: Gray coat, and large broad-brimmed hat.

SULLIVAN, REILLY, MANGAN, AND DOYLE.—A mixed costume, combining the Irish peasant and the smuggler, in various garbs of poverty and ferocity. Ragged pea jackets—Guernsey shirts—loose breeches, with old fisherman's boots over—hairy caps and sou'-westers.

DONOVAN and Farming Peasantry in various garbs.

ARTE O'NEAL.—Neat dress of the present period.

CLAIRE FFOLLIOTT.—*1st Dress*: Fashionable walking-dress. *2nd Dress*: Dark green riding-dress, gilt buttons—black Spanish hat and feathers, gold loop in front.

MRS. O'KELLY.—Black petticoat—brown bedgown—close white cap, fitted to the head, without ribbon or border—spotted handkerchief crossed down her neck—blue stockings—shoes and buckles.

MOYA.—Coloured bodice—smart short petticoat—apron—hair decorated with blue ribbon.

BRIDGET MADIGAN.—Cloak with hood—dark and well-worn drapery beneath it—haybands round the ankles, and highlow boots.

NANCY MALONE.—Irish field peasant—same style in different colours.

IRISH GIRLS.—To correspond in dress with Mrs. O'Kelly.

STAGE DIRECTIONS.

EXITS AND ENTRANCES.—R. means *Right*; L. *Left*; D. F. *Door in Flat*; R. D. *Right Door*; L. D. *Left Door*; S. E. *Second Entrance*; U. E. *Upper Entrance*; M. D. *Middle Door*; L. U. E. *Left Upper Entrance*; R. U. E. *Right Upper Entrance*; L. S. E. *Left Second Entrance*; P. S. *Prompt Side*; O. P. *Opposite Prompt*.

RELATIVE POSITIONS.—R. means *Right*; L. *Left*; C. *Centre*; R. C. *Right of Centre*; L. C. *Left of Centre*.

R.   RC.   C.   LC.   L.

⁎⁎⁎ *The Reader is supposed to be on the Stage facing the Audience.*

THE SHAUGHRAUN.

SCENE I.—*Suil-a-beg.—The Cottage of Arte O'Neal,—The Stage is a Yard in the rear of the Cottage.—The Dairy window is seen facing audience,* R.—*Door 3* E. L., *in return of Cottage.—The ruins of Suil-a-more Castle cover a bold headland in the half distance.—The Atlantic bounds the picture.—Sunset.—Music.*

CLAIRE FFOLLIOTT *at work at a churn,* R. C.

Claire. Phoo! How my arms ache! (*Sings.*)

Where are you going, my pretty maid?
I'm going a-milking, sir, she said.

Enter MRS. O'KELLY (*house,* L.)

Mrs. O'K. Sure, miss, this is too hard work entirely for the likes of you!
Claire. Go on, now, Mrs. O'Kelly, and mind your own business. Do you think I'm not equal to making the butter come?
Mrs. O'K. It's yourself can make the butter come. You have only got to look at the milk and the butter will rise. But, oh, miss! who's this coming up the cliff? It can't be a vision!
(*Looks,* R.)
Claire. 'Tis one of the officers from Ballyragget.
Mrs. O'K. Run in quick, before he sees you, and I'll take the churn.
Claire. Not I!—I'll stop where I am. If he was the Lord Lieutenant himself I'd not stir or take a tuck out of my gown. Go tell the mistress.
Mrs. O'K. And is this the way you will receive the quality?
[*Exit house,* L.
Claire. (*Sings, working.*)

Then what is your fortune, my pretty maid?

He is stopping to reconnoitre. (*Sings again.*)

What is your fortune, my pretty maid?

Here he comes. (*Continues to sing.*)

My face is my fortune, sir, she said.

There's no lie in that, any way; and a mighty small income I've got.

Enter MOLINEUX, 3 E. R., *looking about.*

Mol. My good girl.
Claire. Sir to you. (*Aside.*) He takes me for the dairymaid.
Mol. Is this place called Swillabeg?
Claire. No; it is called Shoolabeg.
Mol. Beg pardon; your Irish names are so unpronounceable. You see, I'm an Englishman.
Claire. I remarked your misfortune. Poor creature, you couldn't help it.
Mol. I do not regard it as a misfortune.
Claire. Got accustomed to it, I suppose. Were you born so?
Mol. Is your mistress at home?
Claire. My mistress. Oh, 'tis Miss O'Neal you mane!
Mol. Delicious brogue—quite delicious! Will you take her my card?
Claire. I'm afeared the butter will spoil if I lave it now.
Mol. What is your pretty name?
Claire. Claire! What's your's?
Mol. Molineux—Captain Molineux. Now, Claire, I'll give you a crown if you will carry my name to your mistress.
Claire. Will you take my place at the churn while I go?
Mol. How do you work the infernal thing?
(*Crosses to her, behind* R.)
Claire. Take hould beside me, and I'll show you. (*He takes handle of churn beside her, they work together.*) There, that's it! Beautiful! You were intended for a dairymaid!
Mol. I know a dairymaid that was intended for me.
Claire. That speech only wanted a taste of the brogue to be worthy of an Irishman.
Mol. (*Kissing her.*) Now I'm perfect.
Claire. (*Starting away.*) What are you doing?
Mol. Tasting the brogue. Stop, my dear; you forget the crown I promised you. Here it is. (*He hands her the money.*) Don't hide your blushes, they become you.
Claire. Never fear, I'll be even wid your honour yet. Don't let—(*up to porch*)—the butther spoil while I'm gone. (*Going, and looking at card.*) What's your name again—Mulligrubs?
Mol. No; Molineux.
Claire. I ax your pardon. You see I'm Irish, and the English names are so unpronounceable.
[*Exit* L. *house.*
Mol. (*Churning gravely.*) She's as fresh and fragrant as one of her own pats of butter. If the mistress be as sweet as the maid, I shall not regret being stationed in this wilderness. Deuced hard work this milk pump! There is a strange refinement about that Irish girl. When I say strange, I am no judge, for I've never done the agricultural shows. I have never graduated in dairymaids, but this one must be the cream of the dairy. Confound this piston-rod; I feel like a Chinese toy!

Enter ARTE O'NEAL (*house* 2 E. L.), *followed by*
CLAIRE.

Arte. What can he want? (*Advancing* L.) What is he doing?

Claire. I have not the slightest idea.
(*Crosses to* R., *behind.*)

Arte. Captain Molineux.

Mol. (*Confused.*) Oh, a thousand pardons! I was just a—amusing myself. I am—a—very fond of machinery, and so—— (*Bows.*) Miss O'Neal, I presume?

Arte. (*Introducing Claire.*) My cousin, Miss Claire Ffolliott.

Mol. Miss Ffolliott! Really I took her for a—— (*Aside.*) Oh, lord! what have I done?

Arte. (*Aside.*) Claire has been at some mischief here.

Claire. (*At churn, and aside to Mol.*) Don't hide your blushes, they become you.

Mol. (*Aside.*) Spare me!

Arte. I hope you come to tell me how I can be of some service to you.

Mol. I have just arrived with a detachment of our regiment at Ballyraggett. The government received information that a schooner carrying a distinguished Fenian hero was hovering about the coast, intending to land her passengers in this neighbourhood. So a gunboat has been sent round to these waters, and we are under orders to co-operate with her. Deuced bore, not to say ridiculous—there is no foundation for the scare—but we find ourselves quartered here without any resources.

Arte. But I regret I cannot extend to you the hospitalities of Suil-a-beg. An unmarried girl is unable to play the hostess.

Claire. Even two unmarried girls couldn't play the hostess.

Mol. But you own the finest shooting in the west of Ireland. The mountains are full of grouse, and the streams about here are full of salmon!

Claire. The captain would beg leave to sport over your domain—shall I spare you the humiliation of confessing that you are not mistress in your own house, much less lady of the manor. (*Up* c.) Do you see that ruin yonder! Oh—'tis the admiration of the traveller, and the study of painters, who come from far and near to copy it. It was the home of my forefathers when they kept open house for the friend—the poor—or the stranger. The mortgagee has put up a gate now, so visitors pay sixpence a head to admire the place, and their guide points across to this cabin where the remains of the ould family, two lonely girls, live. God knows how—you ask leave to kill game on Suil-a-more and Keim-an-eigh. (*Crosses to the dairy window*, 2 E. R.) Do you see that salmon? It was snared last night in the pool a-Bricken by Conn, the Shanghraun. He killed those grouse on daylight on the side of Maurnturk. That's our daily food, and we owe it to a poacher.
(*Down* R.)

Mol. You have to suffer bitterly indeed for ages of family imprudence, and the Irish extravagance of your ancestors.

Arte. Yes, sir, the extravagance of their love for their country, and the imprudence of their fidelity to their faith!

Mol. But surely you cannot be without some relatives!

Claire. I have a brother—the heir to this estate.

Mol. Is he abroad?

Claire. Yes, he is a convict working out his sentence in Australia!

Mol. Oh, I beg pardon. I did not know. (*To Arte.*) Have you any relatives?

Arte. (L.) Yes, I am the affianced wife of her brother!

Mol. (*Confused.*) Really, ladies, I have to offer a thousand apologies.

Arte. I do not accept one—it carries insult to the man I love.

Mol. At least you will allow me do regret having aroused such distressing memories?

Claire. Do you think they ever sleep?

Mol. No!—naturally—of course not—I meant— (*Aside.*) I am astray on an Irish bog here, and every step I take gets me deeper in the mire.
(*Crosses to* L.)

Claire (*Aside.*) How confused he is. That's a good fellow, although he is an Englishman.

Arte. I am very sorry we have not the power to grant you a privilege, which, you see, we do not enjoy.

Kinch (*Outside.*) Holloo! Is there nobody at home? (*Music* 2.)

Arte. Here comes a gentleman who can oblige you.

Kinch. (*Outside.*) Holloo! one of you! Don't you hear me? Bridget come—come and hould my pony.

Mol. Who is this stentorian gentleman?

Claire. Mr. Corry Kinchela; one who has trimmed his fortunes with prudence, and his conscience with economy.

Enter CORRY KINCHELA, 3 E. R.

Kinch. Where the devil is everybody? Oh, there you are! (*Down to* L. C.) I had to stable my own horse! Oh, my service to you, sir!—I believe I've the honour of addressing Captain Molineux. I'm just back from Dublin, and thought I'd stop on my road to tell you the court has decreed the sale of this estate, undher foreclosure, and in two months you'll have to turn out.

Arte. In two months, then, even this poor shelter will be taken from us.

(*Crosses slowly to* R. *of Claire, and down both*, R.)

Kinch. I'm afeard the rightful owner will want to see the worth of his money! But never fear, two handsome girls like yourselves will not be long wanting a shelter—or—a welcome. Eh, captain? oh! ho! It will be pick and choose for them anywhere, I'm thinking.

Mol. (*Aside.*) This fellow is awfully offensive to me.

Kinch. I've been away for the last few weeks, so I've not been able to pay my respects to you officers, and invite you all to sport over this property. You are right welcome, captain. My name is Kinchela—Mr. Corry Kinchela—of Ballyragget House, where I'll be proud to see my tablecloth under your chin. I don't know why one of these girls didn't introduce me.

Mol. They paid me the compliment of presuming that I had no desire to form your acquaintance.
(*Crosses to* C.)

Kinch. What! do you know, sir, that you are talking to a person of position and character?

Mol. I don't care a straw for your position, and I don't like your character.

(*Back turned to Kinchela.*)

Kinch. Do you mean to insult me, sir?
Mol. I am incapable of it.
Kinch. Ah!
Mol. In the presence of ladies; but I believe I should be entitled to do so, for you insulted them in mine. *(Turning to Clare.)* I ask your pardon for the liberty I took with you when I presented myself.
Claire. *(Offering her hand.)* The liberty you took with him when he presented himself clears the account.
Kinch. We'll meet again, sir.
Mol. I hope not. Good evening.
(*To Arte, shaking hands.*)
Arte. I would delay you, captain; but you have a long way across the mountain, and the darkness is falling; the road is treacherous.
[*Molineux goes up to Claire, shakes hands with her again, and exits,
R. 3 E.*

Kinch. The devil guide him to pass the night in a bog-hole up to his neck. Listen hither, you, too. *(Crosses to Claire.)* Sure, I don't want to be too hard upon you. To be sure the sale of this place will never cover my mortgage on it; it will come to me every acre of it. *(Turns to Arte.)* Bedad, the law ought to throw your own sweet self in as a makeweight to square my account. *(She turns away up* c, *he turns to Claire.)* See now, there's your brother, Robert Ffolliott, going to rot over there in Australia, and here in a few weeks you both will be without a roof over your heads. Now, isn't it a cruel thing entirely to let this go on when, if that girl would only say the word, I'd make her Mrs. Kinchela. *(Claire gets to porch.)* And I've got a hoult of the ear of our county member; shure he'll get Robert the run of the country—as free as a fish in a pond he'll be over there. And, stop now—*(To Arte)*—You shall send him a £1,000 that I'll give you on your wedding day.
Arte. I'd rather starve with Robert Ffolliott in a jail than own the county of Sligo if I'd to carry you as a mortgage on it. *(Crosses to* L.*)*
Kinch. *(Down to her).* Do you think the boy cares what becomes of you, or who owns you? Not a haporth! How many letters have you had from him for the last past year!
Arte. *(Up by Claire).* Alas! not one.
Kinch. Not one! *(Aside).* I know that, for I've got them all safe under lock and key. *(Crosses to* R.*, then up to them, aloud.)* See that now; not one thought, not a sign from him, and here I am, every day in the week, like a dog at your door. It is too hard on me entirely. I've some secret schaming behind my back to ruin me entirely in your heart——

Enter FATHER DOLAN, *from house,* L.

I know that it is the same that's sending over to Robert Ffolliott the money, without which he'd starve outright beyant there. I'd like to find out who it is. *(Crosses to* R.*)*
Father D. *(At porch.)* I am the man, Mr. Kinchela!
Kinch. *(Down* R.*)* Father Dolan, may I ask, sir, on what grounds you dare to impache me in the good opinion of these girls?
Father D. Certainly. *(Turns to Arte).* Miss O'Neal—Claire, my dear—will you leave me awhile—(*music,* 3)—alone with Mr. Kinchela; he wants to know the truth about himself.

Claire. And you can't insult him in the presence of ladies. Come, Arte.
[*Arte crosses to door, turns, curtseys to Kinch, and exit. Claire follows, with a look at him.*

Father D. The father of young Ffolliott bequeathed to you and to me the care of his infant son—Heaven forgive me if I grew so fond of my darling charge, I kept no watch over you, my partner, in the trust. Year after year you dipped the estate with your sham improvements and false accounts; you reduced the rents to impoverish the income, so it might not suffice to pay the interest on the mortgages.
Kinch. Go on, sir; this is mighty fine—go on. I wish I had a witness by, I'd make you pay for this. *(Crosses to* L.*)* Is there anything more?
Father D. (R.) There is; you hope to buy the lad's inheritance for an old song when it is sold. Thus you fulfil the trust confided to you by your benefactor, his poor father, whose hand you held when he expired in my arms—thus you have kept the oath to the dead!
Kinch. (L.) Would not every acre of it have escheated to the Crown, as the estate of a convicted felon, only I saved for young Ffolliott by getting his family to make it over before the sentence was pronounced upon him?
Father D. Yes; to make it over to you in trust for these two girls, his sister and his betrothed.
Kinch. To be sure, wasn't you by, and helped to persuade him? More betoken, you were a witness to the deed.
Father D. I was. I helped you to defraud the orphan boy, and since then have been a witness how you have robbed these helpless women. Oh! beware, Kinchela! When these lands were torn from Owen Roe O'Neal in the old times, he laid his curse on the spoilers, for Suil-a-more was the dowry of his bride, Grace Ffolliott. Since then many a strange family have tried to hold possession of the place; but every year one of them would die—the land seemed to swallow them up one by one. Till the O'Neals and Ffolliotts returned none other thrived upon it.
Kinch. Sure that's the raison I want Arte O'Neal for my wife. Won't that kape the ould blood to the fore? Ah, ah, sir! why wouldn't you put in the good word for me to the girl? Do I ask betther than to give back all I have to the family? Sure there's nothing, sir, done that can't be mended that way.
Father D. I'd rather rade the service over her grave, and hear the sods falling on her coffin, than spake the holy words to make her your wife. Corry Kinchela, I know it was by your means and to serve this end, my darling boy—her lover—was denounced and convicted.
Kinch. 'Tis false!
Father D. It is true! But the truth is locked in my soul, and Heaven keeps the key.
(*Up to porch*).
Kinch. (*Aside*.) Some false-hearted cur has confessed again me. (*Aloud.*) Very well, sir. (*Crosses to* R.) Then out of that house these girls shall turn, homeless and beggars.
Father D. Not homeless, while I have a roof over me—not beggars, I thank God, who gives me the crust to share with them.
[*Exit into house,* L.

Kinch. How could he know I had any hand in

bringing young Ffolliott to the dock? Who can have turned tail on me? (To C.)

Enter HARVEY DUFF, 3 E. R.

Harvey D. Whisht, sir!
Kinch. Who's there?—Harvey Duff?
Harvey D. (R. C.) I saw your coppaleen beyant under the hedge, and I knew yourself was in it. I've great news entirely for you—news enough to burst a budget——
Kinch. You are always finding a mare's nest.
Harvey D. I've found one now wid a divil's egg in it.
Kinch. Well, out with it.
Harvey D. There was a fire last night on Rathgarron Head. You know what that means?
Kinch. A signal to some smuggler at sea that the coast is clear, and to run in and land his cargo.
Harvey D. Divil a keg was landed from that ship, barrin' only one man that was put ashore—not a boy was on the strand to meet the boat, nor a car, nor a skip to hurry off the things—only one thing, and that was Conn, the Shaughraun—'twas himself that lighted the signal—'twas him that stud up to his middle in the salt say to carry the man ashore. I seen it all as I lay on the flat of my stomach on the edge of the cliff, and looked down on the pair o' them below.
Kinch. Well, what's all this to me?
Harvey D. Wait, sure. I'm hatching the egg for you. "Who's that," ses I to myself, "that Conn would carry in his two arms as tindher as a mother would hould a child?—who's that," ses I, "that he's capering all around for all the world like a dog that's just onloosed?—who's that he's houlding by the two hands of him, as if 'twas Moya Dolan herself he'd got before him instead of a ragged sailor boy?"
Kinch. Well, did you find out who it was?
Harvey D. Maybe I didn't get snug behind the bushes beside the pathway up the cliff. They passed close to me, talking low; but I heard his voice, and saw the man as plain as I see you now.
Kinch. (C. L.) Saw whom?
Harvey D. (C.) Robert Ffolliott. 'Twas himself I tell you.
Kinch. Are you sure?
Harvey D. Am I sure? Do you think I can mistake the face that turned upon me in the coort when they sentenced him on my evidence, or the voice that said "if there's justice in Heaven, you and I will meet again on this side of the grave?—then," ses he, "have your soul ready," and the look he fixed upon me shrivelled up my soul inside like a boiled cockle that ye might pick out with a pin. Am I sure? I wish I was as sure of Heaven. (To R.)
Kinch. He has escaped from the penal settlement —ay, that's it—and where would he go to straight but he e, into the trap baited with the girl he loves? r

(*Up to cottage, down* L., *and over to* R., *Harvey Duff following him.*)

Harvey D. There'll be a price offered for him, sir—and your honour will put it in my way to airn an honest penny. Wouldn't they hang him this time? Egorra! I'd be peaceable if he was only out of the way for good.
Kinck. Listen to me—D'ye know what took me to Dublin? I heard that the Queen had resolved to release the Fenian prisoners under sentence.
Harvey D. Murther alive—I'm a corpse.

Kinch. I saw the secretary—he mistook my fear for hope—"It is thrue," ses he, "I'm expecting every day to get the despatch, I wish you joy."
Harvey D. Bejabers I'd have liked to seen your face when you got that polthogue in the gob.
Kinch. Robert Ffolliott returned! a free man, he will throw his estates into Chancery.

(To R. *corner.*)

Harvey D. Where will he throw me!
Kinch. He's a fugitive convict still, can't we deal with him?
Harvey D. If his own people around here get to know he's among them, why a live coal in a keg of gunpowdher would not give an "idaya" of the county Sligo.
Kinch. I know it—High and low they love him as they hate me—bad cess to them. (*Crosses* L.)
Harvey D. Oh, nivir fear—he'll keep in the dark for his own sake. (*Music.*)
Kinch. Keep a watch on the Shaughraun—find out where the pair o' em lie in hiding.—Bring me the news to Ballyraggett house—meanwhile, I'll think what's best to be done—Be off, quick! [*Exit Harvey Duff* 3. E. R.] Robert Ffolliott here—tare an' ages—I'm ruined, horse and foot—I'll have all Connaught and the Coort of Chancery on me back. Harvey Duff is right—'tis life or death with me and him—Well, it shall be life with you, Arte O'Neal—and death to him that parts us.

[*Exit* 3. E. R.

SCENE II.—*The Devil's Jowl.*—*A cleft in the rocks on the sea-coast.*

Enter ROBERT FFOLLIOTT, L.

Robert. It must be past the hour when Conn promised to return.—How often he and I have climbed these rocks together in search of the sea-birds' eggs—and waded for cockles in the strand below—Dear faithful truant to ramble with you —how many a lecture from my dear old tutor, Father Dolan, who told me I ought to be ashamed of my love for the Shaughraun. Ah! my heart was not so much to blame after all.
Molineux. (*Outside,* R.) Holloa!
Robert. That's not his voice.
Mol. (*Still outside.*) Holloa!
Robert. Why it's a man in the uniform of an officer—he has seen me. (*Calls.*) Take care, sir—don't take that path—turn to the right—round that boulder—that's the road—Egad, another step and he would have gone over the cliff.—He is some stranger who has lost his way.
Mol. (*Entering.*) What an infernal country!—First I was nearly smothered in a bog, and then, thanks to you my good fellow, I escaped breaking my neck—Do you know the way to Ballyraggett! How far is it to the barracks?
Robert. Two miles.
Mol. Irish miles, of course.
Robert. I shall be happy to show you the road but regret I cannot be your guide. The safest for a stranger is by the cliff to Suil-a-beg.
Mol. But I have just come from there.
Robert. From Suil-a-beg?
Mol. I shall not regret to revisit the place—charming spot—I've just passed there the sweetest hour of my life.
Robert. You saw the lady of the house I presume?
Mol. Pardon me, sir, I mistook your yachting

costume—perhaps you are acquainted with Miss Ffolliott.

Robert. Yes; but we have not met for some time. I thought you referred to Arte—I mean Miss O'Neal.

Mol. Oh! she is charming, of course; but Miss Ffolliott is an angel. She has so occupied my thoughts that I have lost my way—in fact, instead of going straight home, I have been revolving in an obit round that house by a kind of centrifugal attraction, of which she is the centre.

Robert. But surely you admired Miss O'Neal?

Mol. Oh, she is well enough, bright little thing but besides Claire Ffolliott——

Robert. I prefer the beauty of Miss O'Neal.

Mol. I don't admire your taste.

Robert. Well, let us drink to each of them.

Mol. With pleasure, if you can supply the opportunity. (*Robert pulls out his flask, and fills cup.*) Ah! I see you are provided. Allow me to present myself—Captain Molineux, of the 49th. Here's to Miss Claire Ffolliott.

Robert. Here's to Miss Arte O'Neal.
 (*They drink.*)

Mol. I beg your pardon—I did not catch your name.

Robert. I did not mention it. (*A pause.*)

Mol. This liquor is American whisky, I perceive.

Robert. Do you find anything wrong about it?

Mol. Nothing whatever. (*He offers his cup to be filled again.*) But it reminds me of a duty I have to perform. We have orders to capture a dangerous person who will be, or has been, landed on this coast lately, and as these rocks are just the kind of place where he might find refuge——

Robert. Not at all unlikely.—I'll keep a look-out for him.

Mol. I propose to revisit this spot again to-night with a file of men. Here's your health.

Robert. Sir, accept my regards. Here's good luck to you.

Mol. Good night. (*Music 5.—A whistle heard outside.*) What's that?

Robert. 'Tis a ring at the bell. A friend of mine is waiting for me on the cliff above. (*Aside.*) 'Tis Conn!

Mol. Oh, I beg pardon! Farewell.
 [*Going,* R.

Robert. Stop. You might not fare well if you ascend that path alone.

Mol. Why not?

Robert. Because my friend's at the top of it, and if he saw you coming out alone—(*aside*)—he would think I had been caught, and egad! the Shaughraun might poach the Captain!

Mol. Well, if he met me, what then?

Robert. (*Crosses to* R.) You see the poor fellow is mad on one point—he can't bear the sight of one colour, and that is red. His mother was frightened by a mad bull, and the minute Conn sees a bit of scarlet, such, for example, as your coat there, the bull breaks out in him, and he might toss you over the cliff; so, by your leave——

Mol. This is the most extraordinary country I was ever in.

[*Exeunt, arm-in-arm,* L. H. 1 E.

SCENE III.—*Exterior of Father Dolan's Cottage.—Night.—Lighted window.*

Enter MOYA *with pail, which she puts down,* R.

Moya. There! now I've spancelled the cow and fed the pig, my uncle will be ready for his tay. Not a sign of Conn for the past three nights. What's come to him?

Enter Mrs. O'KELLY, L.

Mrs. O'K. Is that yourself, Moya? I've come to see if that vagabond of mine has been round this way.

Moya. Why would he be here—hasn't he a home of his own.

Mrs. O'K. The shebeen is his home when he's not in gaol. His father died o' drink, and Conn will go the same way.

Moya. I thought your husband was drowned at sea?

Mrs. O'K. And, bless him, so he was.

Moya. (*Aside.*) Well, that's a quare way of dying o' drink.

Mrs. O'K. The best of men he was, when he was sober—a betther never dhrawed the breath o' life.

Moya. But you say he never was sober.

Mrs. O'K. Nivir! An' Conn takes afther him!

Moya. Mother.

Mrs. O'K. Well.

Moya. I'm afeard I'll take afther Conn.

Mrs. O'K. Heaven forbid, and purtect you agin him. You are a good, dacent girl, an' desarve the best of husbands.

Moya. Them's the only ones that gets the worst. More betoken yourself, Mrs. O'Kelly.

Mrs. O'K. Conn nivir did an honest day's work in his life—but dhrinkin', an' fishin', an' shootin', an' sportin', and love-makin'.

Moya. Sure, that's how the quality pass their lives.

Mrs. O'K. That's it. A poor man that spoorts the sowl of a gentleman is called a blackguard.

CONN (*Entering* L.)

Conn. There's somebody talking about me.

Moya. (*Running to him.*) Conn!

Conn. My darlin', was the mother makin' little of me? Don't believe a word that comes out o' her! She's jealous—a devil a haperth less. She's choking wid it this very minute, just bekase she sees my arms about ye. She's as proud of me as an ould hen that's got a duck for a chicken. Honld your whist now! Wipe your mouth, an' give me a kiss! (*Crosses to* C.)

Mrs. O'K. (*Embracing him.*) Oh, Conn, what have you been afther? The polis were in my cabin to-day about ye. They say you stole Squire Foley's horse.

Conn. Stole his horse! Sure the baste is safe and sound in his paddock this minute.

Mrs. O'K. But he says you stole it for the day to go huntin'.

Conn. Well, here's a purty thing, for a horse to run away with a man's character like this! Oh, wurra! may I never die in sin, but this was the way of it. I was standing by ould Foley's gate, when I heard the cry of the hounds comin' across the tail end of the bog, and there they wor, my dear, spread out like the tail of a paycock, an' the finest dog fox you'd ever seen saling ahead of them up the boreen, and right across the churchyard. It was enough to raise the inhabitants. Well, as I looked, who should come up and put his head over the gate beside me but the Squire's brown mare, small blame to her. Divil a thing I said to her, nor she to me, for the hounds had lost their scent, we knew by their yelp and whine as they hunted among the grave-stones, when, whish! the fox went by us. I leapt on the gate, an' gave a shriek of a view holloo to the whip; in a minute the pack caught the scent again, an' the whole field came roarin' past. The mare lost her head, an' tore at the gate. "Stop," ses I, " ye devil!" and I slipped the taste of a rope over her head an' into her mouth. Now mind the cunnin' of the baste, she was quiet in a minute. "Come home now," ses I, " asy!" and I threw my leg across her. Be gabers! no sooner was I on her bare back than whoo! holy rocket! she was over the gate, an' tearin' like mad afther the hounds. "Yoicks!" ses I; "come back the thief of the world, where are you takin' me to?" as she went through the huntin' field an' laid me besides the masther of the hounds, Squire Foley himself. He turned the colour of his leather breeches. "Mother of Moses!" ses he, "is that Conn the Shaughraun on my brown mare?" "Bad luck to me!" ses I " It's no one else!" "You sthole my horse,'' says the Squire. "That's a lie!" ses I, "for it was your horse sthole me!"

Moya. An' what did he say to that?

Conn. I couldn't sthop to hear, for just then we took a stone wall and a double ditch together, and he stopped behind to keep an engagement he had in the ditch.

Mrs. O'K. You'll get a month in jail for this.

Coun. Well, it was worth it.

Mrs. O'K. An' what brings you here? Don't you know Father Dolan has forbidden you the house?

Conn. The Lord bless him! I know it well, but I've brought something wid me to-night that will get me absolution. I've left it—(*putting her* L.)— wid the ladies at Suil-a-beg, but they will bring it up here to share wid his riverence.

Mrs. O'K. What is it at all?

Conn. Go down, mother, an' see, an' when you see it, kape your tongue betune your teeth, if one of your sex can.

Mrs. O'K. Well, but you're a quare mortil.

[*Exit* L.

Moya. Oh, Conn! I'm afeared my uncle won't see you. (*Father Dolan inside calls* "Moya.") There! he's calling me. (*Going* R. *taking pail.*)

Conn. Go in an' tell him I'm sthravagin outside till he's soft. Now put on your sweetest lip, darlin'.

Moya. Never fear! sure he does be always telling me my heart is too near my mouth.

Conn. Ah! I hope nobody will ever measure the distance but me, my jewel. (*Music.*)

Moya. Ah! Conn, do you see those flowers? I picked 'em by the way-side as I came along, and I put them in my breast. They are dead already; the life and fragrance have gone out of them; killed by the heat of my heart. So it may be with you, if I picked you and put you there. (*Pause.*) Won't the life go out of your love? hadn't I better lave you where you are?

Conn. For another girl to make a posy of me. Ah,—(*tu'ing pail*) my darling Moya! sure if I was one of th... flowers, and you were to pass me by

like that, I do believe that I'd pluck myself and walk afther you on my own stalk.

[*Exeunt*, R.

SCENE IV.—*A Room in Father Dolan's House. Fireplace* L. *Window at back door,* R. *Lamp on table,* L. C. FATHER DOLAN *reading, sits arm chair,* L.

Father D. What keeps Moya so long outside? Moya!——

Enter MOYA *with tea things, door* R.; *they are on a tray, and she has a kettle in her hand.*

Moya. Yes, uncle, here's your tay, I was waiting for the kettle to boil.

(*Puts things on table, gives Father D. a cup of tea, then to fire with kettle.*)

Father D. I thought I heard voices outside!

Moya. It was only the pig!

Father D. And I heard somebody singing.

Moya. It was the kettle, uncle.

Father D. Go tell that pig not to come here till he's cured, and if I hear any strange kettles singing round here my kettle will boil over.

Moya. Sure uncle! I never knew that happen but you put your fire out. (*At fire kneeling.*)

Father D. See, now, Moya, that ragamuffin Conn will be your ruin. What makes you so fond of the rogue?

Moya. All the batins I got for him when I was a child an' the hard words you gave me since.

Father D. Has he one good quality undher heaven? If he has I'll forgive him.

Moya. He loves me.

Father D. Love! Oh, that word covers more sin than charity. I think I hear it raining, Moya (*she gets* R. *of table*) and I would not keep a dog out in such a night.

Moya. Oh! (*Laughs behind his back.*)

Father D. You may let him stand out of the wet (*Moya beckons on Conn, who enters,* 3 E. R.) but don't let him open his mouth. Gi' me a cup of tay, Moya; I hope it will be stronger than the last.

Moya. Oh! what will I do? He wants his tay stronger, and I've no more tay in the house.

(*A pause. Conn pours whisky into tea-pot. She gives cup of tea.*)

Father D. Well, haven't you a word to say for yourself?

Conn. Divil a one, your riverence!

Father D. You are going to ruin?

Conn. I am, bad luck to me!

Father D. And you want to take a dacent girl along with you. (*Still reading.*)

Conn. I'm a vagabone entirely.

Father D. What sort of a life do you lead? What is your occupation? Stealing salmon out of the river of a night!

(*Puts down book and takes up cup of tea.*)

Conn. No, sir; I'm not so bad as that, but I'll confess to a couple of throut. Sure the salmon is out of saysun.

(*He pulls two trout out of his bag,* L. *of him, and gives them to Moya, who takes them.*)

Father D. And don't you go poaching the grouse on the hill-side.

Conn. I do! divil a lie in it.

(*Pulls out four grouse.*)

Father D. D'ye know where all this leads to?

THE SHAUGHRAUN.

Conn. Well, along with the grouse I'll go to pot.

(*Moya laughs and removes the game and fish. She receives trout on trag from which she has taken the tea-things. She stands on his L. for the trout and R. for the game. Moya returns and busies herself at dresser.*)

Father D. Bless me, Moya!—Moya! this tay is very strong, and has a curious taste.

Conn. Maybe the wather is to blame in regard of being smoked.

Father D. And it smells of whisky.

Conn. It's not the tay you smell, sir, it's me.

Father D. That reminds me. (*Rising, puts down tea and takes up book.*) Didn't you give me a promise last Aister—a blessed promise, made on your two knees—that you would lave off drhink?

Conn. I did, barrin' one thimbleful a day, just to take the cruelty out o' the wather.

Father D. One thimbleful. I allowed that concession, no more.

Conn. God bless ye, ye did; an' I kep' my word.

Father D. Kept your word! how dare you say that! Didn't I find you ten days after stretched out drunk as a fiddler at Tim O'Maley's wake!

Conn. Ye did, bad luck to me!

Father D. And you took only one thimbleful?

Conn. Divil a drhop more—see this. Ah, will ye listen to me, sir? I'll tell you how it was. When they asked me to the wake, I wint—oh, I wouldn't decave you, I wint. There was the Mulcaheys, and the Malones, and the——

Father D. (*Still corner of table, L.*) I don't want to hear about that. Come to the drink——

Conn. Av coorse—egorra! I came to that soon enough. Well, sir, when afther blessing the keeners, and the rest o' 'em, I couldn't despise a drink out of respect for the corpse—long life to it! "But, boys," ses I, "I'm on a puniance," ses I. "Is there a thimble in the house," ses I, "for a divil a dhrop more than the full an it will pass my lips this blessed day."

Father D. Ah!

Conn. Well, as the divil's luck would have it, there was only one thimble in the place, and that was a tailor's thimble, an' they couldn't get it full. (*Father Dolan, to conceal his laughter, goes up, puts his book in recess, then comes down*). Egorra! but they got me full first.

Father D. (*At table.*) Ah, Conn, I'm afeared liquor is not the worst of your doings. We lost sight of you lately for more the six months. In what jail did you pass that time?

Conn. I was on my thravels?

Father D. Where?

Conn. Round the world. See, sir. Afther masther was tuck an' they sint him away the heart seemed to go out o' me entirely. I stand by the say—look over it, an' see the ships sailin' away to where he may be, till the longing grew too big for my body—an' one night I jumped into the coastguard boat, stuck up the sail, and wint to say.

Father D. (L.) Bless the boy, you didn't think you could get to Australia in a skiff.

(*Rises and stands back to fire. Moya gradually down, R.*)

Conn. I didn't think at all—I wint. All night I tossed about, an' the next day and that night, till at daylight I came across a big ship. "Sthop," ses I,—"take me aboard—I'm out of my coorse." They whipped me on deck, an' took me before the Captain. "Where do you come from?" ses he. "Suil-a-beg," ses I. "I'll be obleeged to you to lave me anywhere handy by there." "You'll have to go to Melbourne first," ses he. "Is that anywhere in the County Sligo?" "Why, ye omadhaun," ses he, "you won't see home for six months." Then I set up a wierasthru. "Poor devil," ses the Captain; "I'm sorry for you, but you must cross the ocean. What sort of work can ye do best?" "I can play the fiddle," ses I. "Take him forrad, and be good to him," ses he. An' so they did. That's how I got my passage to Australia.

Father D. You rogue, you boarded that ship on purpose. (*Goes down stage.*)

Moya. (*Coming down, L. C.*) Ay, to get nearer to the young masther. And did you find him, Conn? (*Goes to him.*)

Conn. I did. And oh, sir, when he laid eyes on me, he put his two arums around my neck, an' sobbed an' clung to me like when we were children together. "What brings you here?" ses he. "To bring you back wid me," ses I. "That's impossible," ses he; "I am watched." "So is the salmon in the Glenamoy," ses I; "but I get 'em. So is the grouse on Keim-an-Eigh; but I poach 'em. And now I've come to poach you," ses I. An' I did it. (*Music, 7.*)

Enter ROBERT FFOLLIOTT *with* CLAIRE *and* ARTE, D. R. *Claire down, R.*

Father D. Is this the truth you are telling me? You found him?
(*After an irrepressible gesture, and an inarticulate attempt to bless Conn.*)

Conn. Safe, and in fine condition.
(*Seizes Moya, and stops her mouth as she is about to utter a cry on seeing Robert.*)

Father D. Escaped and free! Tell me——

Conn. Oh, egorra! he must speak for himself now.

Robert. (R.) Father Dolan!
(*Throws off disguise, and embraces him.*)

Father D. Robert, my darling boy! Oh, blessed day! Do I hold you to my heart again?
(*He embraces him*).

Conn. (*Aside to Moya.*) There's nobody looking.
(*Kisses her.*)

Moya. Conn, behave.

Arte. He has been riding on the sea shore among the rocks a whole day and two nights.

Claire. All alone, with sea-weed for his bed.
(*Goes up to fire*).

Moya. Oh, if I'd only known that!

Conn. An' nothin' to eat but a piece of tobacco an' a cockle.

Arte. And he wouldn't stop at Suil-a-beg to taste a morsel; he would come over here to see you.

Father D. Come near the fire. Moya, hurry now, and put food on the table. Sit ye down; let me see you all around me once again. (*Moya brings in food.*) And to think I cannot offer you a glass of wine, nor warm your welcome with a glass of liquor! I have not got a bottle in the house. (*Conn pulls out his bottle, and puts it on the table.*) The rogue——. (*They form a group round the fire.*)

Robert. We may thank poor Conn, who contrived my escape. I made my way across to America.

Claire. But how did you escape, Conn?

Conn. Oh, asy enough; they turned me out.
Arte. Turned you out!
Conn. As if I wor a stray cat. "Very well," says I, "Bally-mulligan is my parish. I'm a pauper; send me, or gi' me board wages where I am. "No," ses they, "we've Irish enough here already." "Then send me back to Sligo," ses I, an' they did.
Claire. They might take you for a cat, for you seem always to fall upon your legs.
Father D. I can't get over my surprise to see my blessed child there sitting by my side. Now, we'll all drink his health.
(*Music. 8. Gives glass to Claire, &c.*)
Conn. Which thimble am I to drink out of?
Father D. The tailor's, you reprobate, are you ready? Now, then—— (*The face of Harvey Duff appears at the window*). Here's his health, and long life to him. May Heaven keep watch over——
Robert. (*His glass in hand* L., *with* R. *slowly pointing to the window.*) Look!—look there.
(*Harvey Duff disappears; they turn*).
Claire. What was it?
Arte. How pale you are!
Robert. The face—I saw the face—there at the window—the same I saw when I was in the dock!
Claire. Ah, Robert, you dream!
Robert. The police spy—Harvey Duff—the man that denounced me. 'Twas his white fact pressed against the glass yonder, glaring at me. [*Exit Conn,* R. 3 E.] Can it be a vision?
(*Father D., up to window.*)
Arte. It was. You are weak, dear; eat—recover your strength.
(*Robert sits* L. *of table—Arte at his feet.*)
Moya. It wasn't a face, but an empty stomach.
Robert. It gave my heart a turn. You must be right. It was a weakness—the disorder of my brain—it must be so.
Father D. The night is very dark. (*Closes curtains —CONN re-enters.*) Well?
Conn. Nothing.
Father D. I thought so. Come, now refresh yourself.
(*Sits on bench, with his back to the audience.*)
Conn. (*Aside.*) Moya, there was somebody there!
Moya. How d'ye know!—did ye see him?
Conn. No; but I left Tatthers outside.
Moya. Your dog. Why didn't he bark?
Conn. He couldn't. I found this in his month.
Moya. What's that?
Conn. The sate of a man's breeches.
[*Exit,* 3 E. R.
Robert. (*Eating.*) My visit here must be a short one. The vessel that landed me is now standing off and on the coast, awaiting my signal to send in a boat ashore to take me away again.
Arte. I am afraid your arrival was expected by the authorities. They are on the watch.
Robert. I know they are. I've had a chat with them on the subject, and a very nice fellow the authority seemed to be, and a great admirer of my rebel sister there.
Claire. Captain Molineux.
(*Crosses to fireplace.*)
Robert. He and I met this morning at the Coot's Nest.
Claire. How dare the fellow talk about me?
Robert. Look at her!—she is all ablaze!—her face is the colour of his coat!
Claire. I never saw the creature but once.
Robert. Then you made good use of your time.

I never saw a man in such a condition; he's not a man—he's a trophy. (*Music,* 9.)
Claire. Robert, you are worse than he is.
Father D. I could listen to him all night.
Arte. So could I.
(*The window is dashed open, Conn leaps in.*)
Conn. Sir—quick—away with yeez—hide!—the red-coats are on us!
Arte. Oh, Robert, fly!
Moya. (R. 3 E.) This way—by the kitchen—through the garden.
Conn. No; the back dure is watched by a couple of them. Is it locked?
Moya. Fast!
Conn. Give me your coat and hat, I'll make a dash out. Tatthers will attend to one, I'll stretch the other, and the rest will give me chase, thinking it is yourself, and then you can slip off unbeknost. (*Three knocks,* D. F.)
Father D. It is too late!
Moya. Hide yourself in the old clock-case in the kitchen. There's just enough room in it for him.
Arte. Quick, Robert, quick! Oh, save yourself if you can!
(*Crosses to* 3 E. R. *Exit with Robert,* D. R.)
Claire. Oh, I wish I was a man, I wouldn't give him up without a fight
(*Crosses to* R. *Exit* 3 E. R.)
Conn. Egorra, the blood of the old stock is in her. (*Standing by* D. F, *with uplifted chair.*) I'm ready, sir. (*Two knocks,* D. F.)
Father D. Conn, put that down, and open the door.

(*Conn opens door.* SERGEANT *and two* SOLDIERS *enter; they stand at door. Sergeant draws window-curtains, and discovers two Soldiers outside, and then exits, saluting* CAPTAIN MOLINEUX *as he enters.*)

Mol. I deeply regret to disturb your household at such an hour, but my duty is imperative.

Enter CLAIRE *and* ARTE, 3 E. R.

A convict escaped from penal servitude has landed on this coast, and I am charged with his capture. Miss Ffolliott, I am sorry to be obliged to perform so painful a duty in your presence, and in yours, Miss O'Neale.
Claire. Especially, sir, when the man you seek is my brother!
Arte. And my affianced husband!
Mol. Believe me, I would exchange places with him, if I could. (L. C.)

Enter *a* SERGEANT, D. F.

Sergeant. (*Saluting.*) Please, sir, there's a mad dog, sir, a-sitting at the back door, and he has bit four of our men awful.
Conn. Tatthers was obliged to perform his painful duty.
Claire. Call off the dog, Conn. Moya, open the back door. (*Crosses to back of table, and gets* L.)
[*Exit Conn, with Moya,* 3 E. R.
Mol. Your assurance gives me hope that we have been misled. (*To* R. C.)
Arte. The house is very small, sir. Here is a bedroom; let your men search it. (*To opening,* L.)

Enter MOYA, CONN, *and two* SOLDIERS, 3 E. R.— *The two Soldiers remain at door,* 3 E. R.

Moya. (*To the two Soldiers.*) I suppose you've

seen there never a human being in my kitchen barrin' the cat? My bedroom is up-stairs—maybe you'd like to search that. (*Down* R.)
Mol. I shall be obliged, sir, to visit every room—sound every piece of furniture, from the roof to the cellar; but the indignity of the proceeding is more offensive to my feelings than it can be to yours. I will accept your simple assurance that the person we are in search of is not in your house. Give me that, and I will withdraw my men.
Claire. (*Offering her hand to* Mol.) Thank you!
(*Goes up* C.)
Arte. (*Aside, to Father Dolan, and* R. *of him.*) Save him, sir! oh, save him!
Father D. (*Aside.*) Oh, God, help me in this great temptation.
Arte. (*Aside, and* L. *of him.*) You will not betray him. Speak—say he is not here!
Mol. I await your reply.
Conn. (*Aside,* R.) I wish he would take my word.
Father D. The lad—the person you seek—my poor boy! Oh, sir, for mercy's sake, don't ask me. He has been here, but——
Mol. He is gone—he went before we arrived?
Arte. Yes—yes! (*Crosses to Claire.*)
Conn. Yes, sir: he wint away before he came here at all.
Mol. Have I your word as a priest, sir, that Robert Ffolliott is not under this roof?
(*Crosses to him.*)
(*Father Dolan, after a passionate struggle with himself, turns from Molineux, and buries his face in his hands.*)

ROBERT *enters,* 3 E. R.

Robert. No, sir. Robert Ffolliott is here!
(*Arte, with a suppressed cry, throws herself into Claire's arms.*)
Mol. I am very sorry for it. (*Goes slowly up to* L. *of Sergeant—Robert crosses, and embraces Father Dolan.*) Secure your prisoner!
(*Claire crosses behind to fireplace—Arte moves a little to the* R.—*Moya drops on stool that she has placed.*)
(*The Sergeant advances,* C.—*Robert meets him, is handcuffed—Sergeant retires two or three paces—Father Dolan totters across, and falls on his knees—Robert raises him, and puts him in chair,* R. *of table—The Sergeant touches Robert on shoulder, then moves to door—Robert is passing out, when Arte throws her arms around his neck.*)
Father D. What have I done?—what have I done? (*Sinking into chair.*)
Conn. Be asy, father. Sure, he'd rather have the iron on his hand, than you the sin upon your sowl!

(*Tableau.—Slow Act Drop.*)

ACT II.

SCENE I.—*Room in Ballyraggett House.—Music.*
Enter KINCHELA *and* HARVEY DUFF, L.
Music.

Kinch. (R.) Come in. How pale you are! Did he resist?

Harvey D. (L.) Give me a glass of sperrets!
Kinch Recover yourself. Is he wounded?
Harvey D. Divil a scratch, but I am.
Kinch. Where?
Harvey D. Nivir mind.
Kinch. You are faint; come and sit down.
Harvey D. No, I'm easier on my feet.
Kinch. How did it happen?
Harvey D. While I was peeping through the keyhole of the kitchen dure.
Kinch. I mean how was he taken?
Harvey D. I did not stop to see, for when he got sight of my face agin the windy, his own turned as white as your shirt. I believe he knew me.
Kinch. Impossible! that black wig disguises you completely. You have shaved off your great red whiskers. Your own mother wouldn't know you.
Harvey D. No, she wouldn't; the last time I went home she pelted me wid the poker. But if the people round here suspected I was Harvey Duff, they would tear me to rags; there wouldn't survive of me a piece as big as the one I left in the mouth of that divil of a dog!
Kinch. Don't be afraid, my good fellow. I'll take care of you.
(*Gets glass and bottle from flat.,* R. *Harvey D, drinks, and returns glass to him before he speaks.*)
Harvey D. And it is yourself you'll be taking care of at the same time. There a pair of us, Misther Kinchela, mind me, now. We are harnessed to the same pole, and as I'm drhuv you must travel.
Kinch. What do you mean?
Harvey D. I mane that I have been your parthner in this game to chate young Ffolliott out of his liberty first, then out of his estate, and now out of his wife! Where's my share?
Kinch Your share! Share of what?
(*Puts away bottle and glass*).
Harvey D. Oh, not the wife. Take her and welcome; but where's my share of the money?
Kinch. Were you not handsomely paid at the time for doing your duty? (*Crosses to* L.)
Harvey D. My jooty! Was it my jooty to come down here among the people disguised as a Fenian delegate, and pass myself off for a head centre, so that I could swear them in an' denounce 'em? Who gave me the office to trap young Ffolliott? Who was it picked out Andy Donovan, an' sent him in irons across the say, laving his young wife to die in a madhouse?
Kinch. Hush! not so loud. (*Crosses to* R.)
Harvey D. Do you remember the curse of Bridget Madigan, when her only boy was found guilty on my evidence? Take your share of that, an' give me some of what I have airned.
Kinch. You want a share of my fortune?
Harvey D. A share of our fortune!
Kinch. (R.) Every penny I possess is invested in this estate. If Robert Ffolliott returns home a free man I could not hould more of it than would stick to my brogues when I was kicked out. Listen to this letter that I found here to-night waiting for me. It is from London. (*Reads.*) "On Her Majesty's service. The Home Office. In reply to your inquiries concerning Robert Ffolliott, undergoing penal servitude, I am directed by his lordship to inform you that Her Majesty has been pleased to extend a full pardon to the Fenian prisoners."
Harvey D. Pardoned! I'm a corpse!

Kinch. (*Reads.*) "But as Robert Ffolliott has effected his escape, the pardon will not extend to him unless he should reconstitute himself a prisoner."
Harvey D. Oh, lor'! that is exactly what he has done. He has gave himself up.
Kinch. Was he not captured?
Harvey D. No bad luck to it. Our schame to catch him has only qualified him for a pardon.
Kinch. What! has an infernal fate played such a trick upon me?
Harvey D. The divil will have his joke.
Kinch. His freedom and return here is your death warrant and my ruin. (*To* R.)
Harvey D. I'll take the next ship to furrin parts. (*To* L.)
Kinch. Stay! the news is only known to ourselves.
Harvey D. In a couple of days it will be all over Ireland, and they will let him out! Tare alive! what'll I do? Where will I go? I'll swear an information against meself, and get sent to jail for purtection.
Kinch. Listen, I've a plan. Can I rely upon your help?
Harvey D. I'll do anything short of murder, but I'll get somebody to do that for me. What's to be done?
Kinch. (*Close to Harvey D.*) I'll visit him in prison, and offer him the means to escape. Now what more likely than he should be killed while making the attempt?
Harvey D. Oh! whew! the soldiers will not dhraw a trigger on him barrin' a magistrate is by to give the ordher.
Kinch. But the police will. You will go at once to the police-barracks at Sligo, pick your men, tell 'em you apprehend an attempt at rescue. The late attack on the police-van at Manchester, and the explosion at Clerkenwell prison in London will warrant extreme measures.
Harvey D. The police won't fire if he doesn't defend himself.
Kinch. But he will!
Harvey D. Where will he get the arms?
Kinch. I will provide them for him!
Harvey D. Corry Kinchela, the divil must be proud of you!
Kinch. We must get some of our own people to help, and if the police hesitate, sure it's the duty of every loyal subject to kill a fugitive convict. What men could we depend on at a pinch?
Harvey D. There's Sullivan an' Doyle.
Kinch. Which Doyle?
Harvey D. Jim Doyle.
Kinch. Jim Doyle!
Harvey D. Yes, the man with the big carbuncle on the end of her nose. Then there's Reilly.
Kinch. Reilly? He's transported.
Harvey D. No, no; he's not.
Kinch. Oh, but he will, and you'll be hanged.
Harvey D. And so will you—an' Mangan, an' all their smuggling crew.
Kinch. Where can you find them?
Harvey D. At the Coot's Nest. They expect a lugger in at every tide.
Kinch. Have them ready and sober to-night. Come to me for instructions at midday. (*Going—stops.*) Ah! that will do—he will fall into that trap—(*rubs his hands*)—it can't fail.
[*Exit,* R.
Harvey D. (*Speaking after Kinch's exit.*) Harvey Duff, take a friend's advice—get out of this place as quick as you can. Take your little pickin's and your passage across the salt say; find some place where a rogue can live peaceably—have some show and a chance of making an honourable living.
[*Exit* L.—*Scene changes. Music.*

SCENE II.—*Parlour at Father Dolan's—(as before.)*
Father D. at fireside. Claire looking out of window; window curtains open. Curtains of opening closed.

Father D. There, my darling, do not sob so bitterly. Sure that will do no good, and only spoil your blue eyes.
Arte. What's the good of my eyes if I can't see him. Let me cry. God help me! what else can I do? Oh, if I could only see him—speak to him—one minute! Do you think they would let me in?
Father D. I have sent a letter to the Captain. Moya has carried it to the barracks.
Arte. If Claire had gone instead of Moya—had she pleaded for us, he would not refuse her.
Claire. But I could not go.
Arte. Why not?
Claire. I could not ask that Englishman a favour.
Father D. You speak unkindly and unjustly. He acted with a gentle forbearance, and a respect for my character and our sorrow, I cannot forget.
Claire. Nor can I?
Father D. It made a deep impression on my heart.
Claire. Yes; a bitter curse on the day I ever laid eyes on him. (*Coming down* R.)
Arte. (*Rising, and down to her behind table.*) Oh, Claire, you wrong him! Surely I have no cause to regard him as a friend; but you did not see the tears in his eyes when I appealed to his mercy——
Claire. Didn't I?
Father D. (*Still seated.*) Poor fellow, he suffered for what he was obliged to do. You should not hate the man.
Claire. (*Up.*) I don't! And that's what ails me!
Arte. Are you mad?
Claire. (*Down*) I am! I've tried to hate him, and I can't! Do you think I was blind to all you saw? I tried to shut my eyes; but I only shut him in. I could not shut him out! I hate his country and his people.
(*Crosses to* L. *Arte to table.*)
Father D. You were never there.
Claire. (L.) Never! and I wish they had never been here, particularly this fellow, who has the impudence to upset all my principles with his chalky smile and bloodless courtesy. I can't stand the ineffable resignation with which he makes a fool of himself and me. (*Father D. goes to fire, and MOYA enters,* D. F. R.) (*Eagerly.*) Well, have you seen him? Can't you speak?
Moya. I will when I get my breath. Yes, I saw him, and, oh! how good and——
Claire. (L.) Stop that! we know all about that! Where is his answer?—quick!
Moya. (R.) He's bringing it himself!
Claire. Oh! (*Turns away.*) We don't want him here. (*To window.*)
Arte. (C.) Did you see the young master?
Moya. No, miss; nobody was let in to see him.
Father D. What kept you so long then?
Moya. Conn come back wid me (*Arte gets in front of table*), and knowing you did not want him round

here, I was thrying to get away from him—that's what kept me; but he was at my heels all the way, and Tatthers at his heels. A nice sthreel we made along the road.
Father D. Where is he?
Moya. They are both outside.
Father D. The pair of vagabonds? Why does he not go home?
Moya. (*Going up* R.) He says the ould woman is no consolation.
Conn. (*Sings outside.*)

"If I were dead an' in my grave,
No other tombstone would I have
But I'd dig a grave both wide and deep,
With a jug of punch at my head and feet.
 "Ri tooral loo."

Father D. Is the fellow so insensible to our sorrow that he sets it to the tune of a jug of punch?
Claire. Don't blame poor Conn. The boy is so full of sport that I believe he would sing at his own funeral. (*At desk.*)
Moya. Long life to ye, miss, for the good word.
Conn. (*Entering*, 3 E. R., *and speaking to his dog.*) Lie down now, an' behave.
Father D. Where have you been all night?
Conn. Where would I be but undher his prison windy, keeping up his heart wid the songs and the divarshin!
Arte. Diversion. (*Father D., down to Arte.*)
Conn. Sure I had all the soldiers dancing to my fiddle, and I put Tatthers through all his thricks. I had 'em all in fits of laffin' when I made him dance to my tunes. That's the way the masther knew I was waiting on him. He guessed what I was at, for when I struck up "Where's the slave?" he answered inside with "My lodging is on the cowld ground;" then when I made Tatthers dance to "Tell me the sorrow in my heart"—till I thought they'd have died wid the fun—he sung back "The girl I left behind me," mainin' yourself, Miss Arte, an' I purtended that the tears runnin' down my nose was with the laffin'.
(*Moya puts stool by Conn. Wipes his eyes with apron.*)
Father D. I did you great wrong. I ask your pardon.
Arte. What is to be done?
Conn. I've only to whisper five words on the cross-roads and I'd go bail I'd have him out of that before night.
Father D. Yes; you would raise the country to attack the barracks, and rescue him. I will not give countenance to violence.
(*Crosses to* L. *with Arte.*)
Claire. 'Tis the shortest way out!
Arte. Oh, any way but that!
Moya. (*Aside to Conn, taking up stool.*) Come into my kitchen. Have you had nothin' to ate since yesterday?
Conn. Yes, my heart, I've that in my mouth all the night.
[*Exit, with Moya,* 3 E. R.
Claire. (*Who is watching at window.*) Here he comes.
(*A knock. After Molineux pass window, Claire crosses, and sits by fire, back to audience.*)
Father D. There's a knock at the door.
Arte. 'Tis he!
Claire. I know that.

Father D. Why did you not let him in?
(*Crosses to door.*)
Claire. (*Aside.*) Because I was trying to keep him out.
(*Father D. opens door. Molineux enters* D. F. R. *Arte to front of table.*)
Mol. Good day, sir. I ventured to intrude in person to bring you this order, necessary to obtain admission to see Mr. Ffolliott, and that I might entreat you to bear me no ill-will for the painful duty I had to perform last night.
(*Hands a paper to Arte.*)
Claire. Oh, no, sir; you had to deprive us of a limb, and I suppose you performed the operation professionally well. Do you come for your fee in the form of our gratitude?
Father D. Forgive her, sir! Claire, this is too bad!
Mol. (*Awkward.*) Oh, no—not at all! Pray don't mention it—I assure you.
Arte. This paper is signed by Mr. Kinchela—are we indebted to him for the favour?
Mol. The prisoner is now in the custody of the civil power, and Mr. Kinchela is the magistrate of the district.
Father D. (*Taking his hat from desk.*) Come, Arte. Come, Claire.
Arte. (*To Mol.*) We are grateful—(*giving hands*)—very grateful for your kindness in our affliction. (*Aside to Mol., and pointing to Claire.*) Don't mind her.

[*Father D. takes Mol.'s hand, and then exit with Arte,* D. F. R.
Mol. (*Aside.*) Don't mind her; I wish I did not. (*Aloud.*) May I be permitted to accompany you to——
(*Advances to upper corner* R. *of table, and puts down cap.*)
Claire. (*Still seated.*) To the prison? Do you wish to make the people about here believe I am in custody. A fine figure I'd make hanging on the arm of the policeman who arrested my brother!
Mol. You cannot make me feel more acutely than I do the misery of my condition. I did not sleep a wink last night.
Claire. And how many winks do you suppose I got?
Mol. I tried to act with as much tenderness as the nature of my duty would permit.
Claire. That's the worst part of it.
Mol. Do you reproach me with my gentleness?
Claire. I do! You have not even left us the luxury of complaint.
Mol. Really, I don't understand you.
Claire. No wonder. I don't understand myself!
(*Rising, and at fire.*)
Mol. Well, if you don't understand yourself, you shall understand me, Miss Ffolliott. You oblige me to take refuge from your cruelty, and place myself under the protection of your generosity. You extort from me a confession that I feel is premature, for our acquaintance has been short.
Claire. And not sweet.
Mol. I ask your pity for my position last night, when I found myself obliged to arrest the brother of the woman I love.
Claire (*At* L. *of table.*) Captain Molineux, do you mean to insult me? Oh, sir, you know I am a friendless girl, alone in this house—my brother in a jail! I have no protection!
Mol. Miss Ffolliott—Claire!

Enter CONN, *followed by* MOYA, 3 E. R.

Conn. Did you call, miss?
Claire. (*After a pause.*) No. (*Turns to* L.)
Conn. I thought I heard a screech. (*Music.*)
Claire. Go away; I don't want you.
(*To corner,* L.)
Moya. (*Aside to Conn.*) Don't you see what's the matther?
Conn. No.
Moya. You're an omadhaun. Come out of that, an' I'll tell you.
[*Exit with Conn,* 3 E. R. *Claire crosses to* R, *then to bench, sits face to audience, handkerchief to face.*

Claire. There! what will those pair think of us? Do you see what you have exposed me to? Is it not enough to play the character of executioner of my brother, but you must add to your part this scene of outrage on me!
(*Sits down, and weeps passionately.*)
Mol. Forgive me. I ask it most humbly. If I said I would give my heart's blood to the last to spare you one of those tears, you might feel the avowal was an offence. What can I say? Miss Ffolliott, for mercy sake don't cry so bitterly!—forget what I've done! (*Front of table.*)
Claire. I—I can't!
Mol. On my knees, I implore your pardon. I'll go away. I'll never see you again. (*Claire suddenly and mechanically arrests his movement by catching his arm. Mol. kisses her hand.*) Heaven bless you—farewell!
Claire. (*Without moving her hands from face.*) Don't go.
Mol. (*Advances a little.*) Did I hear right? You bid me stay?
Claire. Am I mad? (*Rises, and goes to fireplace.*)
Mol. Miss Ffolliott, I am here.
Claire. I forgive you on one condition.
Mol. I accept it, whatever it may be.
Claire. Save my brother.
Mol. I'll do my best. Anything else?
Claire. Never speak of love to me again.
Mol. (*Close to her.*) Never, never! On my honour I will never breathe a——
Claire. Until he is free.
Mol. And then may I—may I——
(*He stands beside her at fireplace; her head bent down, he steals his arm around her.*)

Claire. Not a word until then.
Mol. Not a word!
(*Claire leans her head on his shoulder. Slow close in, as he kisses her.*)

SCENE III.—*Room in the Barracks.*

Enter the SERGEANT, *followed by* KINCHELA, L.

Kinch. I am Mr. Kinchela, the magistrate. I wish to see the prisoner; he must be removed to police quarters.
Sergeant. We shall be glad to get rid of him.—It is the police business. Our men don't half like it.
[*Exit,* R.
Kinch. Now I'll know at once by his greeting whether those girls have been speakin' about me.
(*Goes to* L.)

Enter ROBERT, *followed by* SERJEANT, R., *who crosses to* L.

Robert. Kinchela, my dear friend, I knew you would not fail me.
Kinch. (*Aside.*) 'Tis all right. (*Turns coldly, and with stiff manner.*) Pardon me, Mr. Ffolliott, you forget your position and mine—I bear Her Majesty's commission as justice of the peace, and whatever friendship once united us it ceased when you became a rebel.
Robert. Do I hear aright? Your letters to me breathed the most devoted——
Kinch. (*To Sergeant.*) You can leave us. (*Sergeant goes out* L.—*he suddenly changes his manner.*) My dear young master, forgive me, in the presence of that fellow I was obliged to play the magistrate.
Robert. (R.) Egad! you took my breath away.
Kinch. (L.) Didn't I do it well—my devotion to you and the precious charge you left in my care exposes me to suspicion. I am watched, and to preserve my character for loyalty I am obliged to put on airs—Oh! I'm your mortal enemy, mind that.
Robert. You!
Kinch. Every man, woman, an' child in the county Sligo believes it, and hate me. I've played my part so well that your sister an' Miss O'Neal took offence at my performance.
Robert. No—ha! ha!
Kinch. Yes! ho! ho! they actually believe I am what I am obliged to appear, and they hate me cordially. I'm the biggest blackguard——
Robert. You! my best friend!
Kinch. Oh, I don't mind it! The truth is, I'm afeard if I had betrayed my game to them—you know the weakness of the sex—they could not have kept my secret.
Robert. But surely Father Dolan?
Kinch. He is just as bad.
Robert. Forgive them.
Kinch. I do.
Robert. The time will come when they will repent their usage of you.
Kinch. Ay, by my soul it will.
Robert. They have no friend, no protector but you; for now my chains will be more firmly riveted than ever.
Kinch. Whisht! you must escape.
Robert. It is impossible! How? When?
Kinch. To-night! To-morrow, when you are removed to Sligo jail, it might not be so aisy; but to-night I can help you.
Robert. To regain my freedom?
Kinch. Is that ship that landed you within reach?
Robert. Every night at eight o'clock she runs in shore, and lies-to off the coast; a bonfire lighted on Rathgarron Head is to be the signal for her to send off her skiff under the ruins of St. Bridget's Abbey to take me on board.
Kinch. That signal will be fired to-night, and you shall be there to meet the boat.
Robert. Do you, indeed, mean this, Kinchela? Will you risk this for my sake?
Kinch. I will lay down my life if you want it.
(*They embrace.*)
Robert. What am I to do?
Kinch. Give me your promise that you will not breathe a word to mortal about the place I am going to propose; neither to your sister, nor to Miss O'Neal, nor, above all, to Father Dolan.

Robert. Must I play a part to deceive them?
(*Crosses to* L.)
Kinch. My life and liberty are staked in the attempt as well as yours.
Robert. I give you the promise.
Kinch. To-night your quarters will be changed to the old Gate Tower. Wait till dark, then use this chisel to pick out the stones that form the back of the fireplace in your room. The wall there is only one course thick.
(*He gives Robert chisel.*)
Robert. You are sure?
Kinch. Conn, the Shaughraun, was shut up in that cell last spring, and he picked his way out through the wall with a two-pronged fork. He was creeping out of the hole he had made when they caught him. The wall has been rebuilt, but the place has not served as a prison since.
Robert. Where shall I find myself when I am outside?
Kinch. In a yard enclosed by four low walls. There's a door in one of them that's bolted on the inside. Open that, and you are free.
Robert. Are there no sentinels posted there?
Kinch. No; but if there is, there's a double-barrelled pistol that will clear your road. (*Hands pistol.*)
Robert examines it.) (*Aside.*) I'll put Duff outside that door; there'll be an end to him.
Robert. (*Returning the pistol.*) Take it back. I will not buy my liberty at the price of any man's life. I will take my chance; but, stay, the signal on Rathgarron Head! Who will light the bonfire? (*Conn playing outside.*) Hark!—'tis Conn! Do you hear? Poor fellow! he is playing "I'm under your window, darling." Ah! I can employ him. How will he do it?—how will I send him word?
Kinch. You won't betray me?
Robert. No, no. (*Writes in his book—repeats as he writes.*) "Be at Rathgarron Head to-night, beside the tar barrel." What signal can I give him that he will be able to hear or see across the bay?
Kinch. (*Dictating.*) "When you hear two gunshots on St. Bridget's Abbey, light the fire."
Robert. (*Writes.*) "When you hear two gunshots——" For that purpose I accept it.
Kinch. (*Gives Robert the pistol.—Aside.*) No matter for what purpose. He will use it to serve mine. If they hang him for murdering Harvey Duff, I'll be afther killing two birds wid one stone.
Robert. Beg the sentry to come here.
Kinch. What are you going to do?
Robert. You will see.
(*Taking out coins.*)
Kinch. Here is the Sergeant.
(*He enters* L.)
Robert. (*Folding money in the paper.*) Will you give these few pence to the fiddler outside, and beg the fellow to move on?
(*Hands paper to Sergeant.*)
Sergeant. The men encourage him about the place. (*Going.*) There's Father Dolan and Miss O'Neal outside; they have got a pass to see you.
Robert. Show them in.
[*Exit Sergeant,* L.
Kinch. Now, watch their manner towards me; but you won't mind a word they say against me.
Robert. (L.) Not I. I know you better. (*Fiddle outside.*) Hush! 'tis Conn. He has got the letter. Listen—"I'll be faithful and true!" Ay, as the ragged dog at your heels is faithful and true to you, so you have been to me, my dear, devoted, loving playfellow—my wild companion!

Enter ARTE *and* FATHER DOLAN, L.

Arte. Robert! (*Embracing him.*) Mr. Kinchela!
Father D. I am surprised to find you here, sir!
Kinch. (*Aside to Robert.*) D'ye hear?
Robert. (*Aside to Kinch.*) All right!
Arte. You do not know that man.
Kinch. Oh, yes he does. I've made a clane breast of it.
Robert. Yes, he has told me all.
Kinch. How I brought all of you to ruin, and betrayed my trust—(*Crossing to* L.)—and grew rich and fat on my plunder. I defy you to make me out a bigger blackguard than I've painted myself, so my sarvice to you!
[*Exit* L.
Father D. (L.) When St. Patrick made a clean sweep of all the venomous reptiles in Ireland, some of the vermin must have found refuge in the bodies of such men as that.
Robert. This is the first uncharitable word I ever heard you utter.
Father D. Heaven forgive me for it, and him! You're right, my vocation is to pray for sinners, not revile them.
Arte. And mine to comfort you, and not to bring our complaints to add to your misfortune.
Robert. (*Crossing to* c.) Hold up your hearts; mine is full of hope.
Father D. Hope; where do you find it?
Robert. In her eyes! You might as well ask me where I find love. I was in prison when I stood liberated on American soil. The chains were on my soul when I stretched it longing across the ocean towards my home; but now I am in prison, this narrow cell is Ireland. I breathe my native air, and am free!
Father D. They will send you back again.
Arte. (R.) Ah, sure! the future belongs to heaven, the present is our own.
Father D. I believe I was wrong to come here at all. I feel like a mourning band on a white hat!
(*Music.*)

SERGEANT (*Entering* L.)

Sergeant. Sorry to disturb you, sir, but we are ordered to shift your quarters. You will occupy the room in the Old Gate Tower. The guard is waiting, sir, when you are ready.
[*Exit,* R.
Robert. I am prepared to accompany you.
Arte. Must we leave you?
Robert. For the present, but we shall soon meet again. Now will you indulge a strange humour of mine? You know the ruins of St. Bridget's Abbey, where we have so often sat together?
Arte. Can I ever forget it! We go there often; the place is full of you.
Robert. Go there to-night at nine o'clock.
Arte. I'll offer up a prayer at the old shrine.
Robert. Ay, with all my heart, for I may want it.
Father D. What do you mean? There's some mischief going on; I know it by his eye. He used to wear the same look when he was going to give me the slip and be off from his Latin grammar to play truant with Conn the Shaughraun.
Robert. Ask me nothing, for I can answer you only one word—hope!

Father D. 'Tis the finest word in the Irish language.
Arte. There's a finer—faith!
(*Embraces Robert.*)
Father D. And love is the mother of those heavenly twins. I declare my heart is lifted up between you, as if your young ones were its wings.
(*Backs up stage a little.*)
Robert. Good night, and not for the last time.

SERGEANT enters, R.

Arte. Good night!
Father D. I leave my heart with you. God bless you!
(R. *hand to Rob.*)
Robert. Remember, to-night at the Abbey.
Arte. (*Aside.*) At nine o'clock.
Robert. I shall be there. (*She utters an exclamation.*) Hush! [*Exit Father D. with Arte, L.*] You gave the money to the fiddler?
Sergeant. Yes, sir!
Robert. (*Aside, crosses to* R.) Ah, I forgot! Conn can't read. What will he do to decipher, my note?—bah! I must trust to his cunning to get at the contents. Now, sergeant, lead me to my new cell in the Gate Tower.
[*Exeunt,* R.

SCENE IV.—Mrs. O'Kelly's Cabin.—Exterior.—Evening.

Conn. (*Entering with a paper in his hand,* R.) There's writing upon it. Himself has sent me a letther. Well, this is the first I ever got, and well to be sure, (*Looks at it—turns it over.*) I'd know more about it if there was nothing in it; but it's the writin' bothers me.
Mrs. O'K. (*Entering,* D. F. R.) Is that yourself, Conn?
Conn. (*Aside.*) I wish it was somebody else that had book larnin'.
Mrs. O'K. What have you there?
Conn. It's a letther the masther is afther writin' to me.
Mrs. O'K. What's in it?
Conn. Tuppence was in it for postage. (*Aside.*) That's all I made out of it.
Mrs. O'K. I mane what does he say in it?
Conn. Rade it!
Mrs. O'K. You know I can't.
Conn. Oh, ye ignorant ould woman!
Mrs. O'K. I know I am; but I took care to send you to school, Conn, though the sixpence a week it cost me was pinched out of my stomach and off my back.
Conn. The Lord be praised that ye had it to spare, anyway.
Mrs. O'K. Go on, now—it's makin' fun of yer ould mother ye are. Tell me what the young masther says.
Conn. In the letther?
Mrs. O'K. Yes!
Conn. (*Aside.*) Murther, what'll I do? (*Aloud.*) Now, mind, it's a sacret. (*Reads.*) "Collee costhum garanga caravat selibubu luckli rastuck pig."
Mrs. O'K. What's that—it's not English!
Conn. No; it's in writin'—now kape that to yourself.
Claire. (*Entering,* R.) Conn, there is some project on foot to-night to rescue my brother—don't deny it—he has almost confessed as much to Father Dolan. Tell me the truth!
Conn. I would not decaive you Well, I promised not to say a word about it; but there it is, rade it for yourself.
(*Crosses to* C.)
Claire. (*Looks at note.*) Yes; 'tis his hand.
Conn. I knew it in a minute.
Claire. It is in pencil!
Conn. (*To Mrs. O'K.*) I told you it wasn't in English.
Claire (*Reads.*) "Be at Rathgarron Head to-night beside the tar-barrel. When you hear two gun-shots in St. Bridget's Abbey, light the fire."
Conn. You wouldn't believe me when I read that to you ten minutes ago. The signal fire, that's to tell the ship out at sea beyant there to send a boat ashore to take him off.
Mrs. O'K. Oh, blessed day! Is it to escape from gaol he'd be thrying?
Claire. He has told my cousin to be in the ruins to-night.
Conn. There's going to be a scrimmage, an' I'm not in it. I'm to be sent away like this. It's too hard on me intirely. Oh, if I could find somebody to take my place and fire the signal! I'd bring him out of gaol this night if I had to tear a hole in the wall wid my five fingers!
Claire. I'll take your place!
Conn. You will!
Mrs. O'K. (*Crosses to* C.) Oh, Miss Claire, don't go; there'll be gun-shots and bagginets! This is one of Conn's divilments, and ye'll be all murthered! Oh, weir asthru! what'll I do?
Conn. Will ye hould your whisht?
Mrs. O'K. No, I won't! I'll go an' inform agin ye before ye get into throuble, and then, mayle, they'll let you off aisy.
Claire (*Crosses to* L.) Here comes the Captain. For Heaven's sake, pacify her! She will betray us.
Conn. Well, come inside, mother, darlin'! There! I'll stop wid ye. Will that aise your mind? You onsensible ould woman!
Mrs. O'K. (R.) Conn, don't lave me alone in the world! Sure, I've nobody left but yourself, an' if ye're taken from me, I'll be a widdy!
Conn. Then both of us will be two widdys together. Don't ye hear Miss Claire is going to take my place?
Mrs. O'K. (*Crosses to* C.) Heaven bless an' purtect every hair of your head, miss! And will ye, indeed, spend one night by the mother's fireside?
Conn. And I'll play all the tunes you love best on my fiddle till I warm the cockles of your ould heart!
(*Sings.*)

"Oh, then, Conn, my son, was a fine young man,
An' to every one cuish he had one shin;
Till he wint to the wars of a bloody day,
When a big cannon-ball whipped his two shins away,
An' my rickety a——"
[*Exeunt.*

Enter ARTE and MOLINEUX, L.

Arte. I have invited the Captain to pass the evening at Suil-a-beg, but he will not be persuaded.
Mol. I may not desert my post till the police arrive from Sligo to relieve me of my charge.
Arte. But your soldiers are there?
Mol. Soldiers will not move without orders, besides, my men have such a distaste for this business, that I believe, if left to defend their prisoner against an attempt to rescue him, they would disgrace themselves.

THE SHAUGHRAUN. 17

Arte. (*Aside to Claire.*) Get him away; an attempt will be made to-night.
(*Crosses to* R.)
Claire. (*Aside.*) Leave us!
Arte. Well, good day, Captain. Come Claire.
[*Exit* R.
Claire. (*After a pause.*) It is a lovely evening.
(*Going* R.)
Mol. You are not going home.
Claire. Not yet. I shall take a stroll along the shore to Rathgarron Head!
Mol. Alone?
Claire. I suppose so!
Mol. Is it far?
Claire. No!
Mol. Not far—ahem! would you allow me to go part of the road beside you? (*Music.*)
Claire. Pray do not neglect your duty on my account, besides I want to consult my feelings in solitude uninfluenced by your presence.
Mol. That sweet confession gives me hope and courage.
Claire. Good night! leave me, light a meditative cigar, and go back to your duty. (*He takes out cigar-case.*) Leave me to wander by the light of the rising moon, and sit down on the rocks beside the sea.
(*He takes match—she lights one and keeps the box.*)
Mol. How good you are!—an angel!
Claire. Of light. There, good night!
Mol. Good night! (*She goes off very slowly* R. *He moves away—turns.*) Oh, if I had some excuse to follow her a little way. (*He brushes the light away from the end of his cigar, and calls.*) Miss Ffolliott, pardon me, but my cigar is out, and you have my matches—ha! ha! sorry to trouble you, oh, don't come back, I beg. (*Follows her out* R.)
Conn. (*Leaping out of window and fastening shutters.*) I've locked the dure an' barred the shutters!
Mrs. O'K. (*Inside.*) Conn, let me out!
Conn. Behave now, or I'll tell the neighbours you've been drinking. Good night, mother!
(*Runs out* R.)

SCENE V.—*The interior of prison, large window* R. *old fireplace* R. C., *small window* C., *door* L. *Through window* R. *is seen exterior and court-yard—night.*

Robert. (*Discovered listening,* D. L.) They are relieving guard. (*Drum.*) I shall not receive another visit for the night. Now to work—that must be the wall Kinchela spoke of. I see some new brick-work there, but where shall I land? Is there much of a drop into the yard below? (*Looks out of window* R.) The wall hides the interior—can reach this window?
(*Climbs to window* L. *as Conn is seen at window* R.)
Conn. Divil a sowl about this side of the tower. There's a light in his cell. I wondher is he alone? No matter. Where's my iron pick? Now to make a hole in the wall. (*Disappears.*)
Robert. The yard seems to be on a level of this chamber. Where's my chisel? (*Begins to work.*) The mortar is as soft as butter. This was done by government contract. It's an ill wind that blows nobody any——What's that? It sounds like somebody at work on the wall. Can it be a rat? (*Listens.*) No, it stops now. (*He works.*) There it goes again. [*He stops.*) Now it stops. It echoes me as if there was some one on the other side. Oh, Lord! my heart sinks at the thought. I'll satisfy myself.
(*He goes to window,* L.)
Conn. (*Appearing at window,* R.) There's a rat in the chimbley! Gorra! maybe I'm all wrong, and himself is not in it at all.
(*Looks in at window as Robert, having climbed, looks out* L.)
Robert. I can't see round the corner, but there seems to be no one there.
Conn. Divil a sowl in it. I wish I could see crooked. Here goes again. (*Disappears* L.)
Robert. The noise has ceased—it was a rat. (*Works.*) This brick is loose enough to pull out; but if that goes, the rest seem shaky. They will fall together. (*A mass of brickwork falls, and discovers Conn.*) Conn!
Conn. Whisht! Who the devil would it be? Asy, for the love of Heaven, now! Come asy! I've left Tatthers in the guard-room with the men. Stop till I break another coorse of bricks for ye.
(*The scene moves—pivots on a point at the back. The Prison moves off and show the exterior of Tower with Conn clinging to the walls, and Robert creeping through the orifice. The walls of the Yard appear to occupy three-fourths of stage.*)

Enter KINCHELA, HARVEY DUFF, *and four* CONSTABULARY, 3 E. R. *Conn and Robert disappear into the Yard.*

Kinch. Whisht! there's a noise in the yard! This door is boulted on the inside; but there's a pile of rubbish shot against the back wall that we can see over. (*To Harvey Duff.*) Harvey Duff, you will stand there; the rest come with me.
(*Kinch and four Constabulary go up,* R, *and disappear behind wall. Harvey Duff, holding a short carbine ready, stands* R. *of door with his back to wall.*)
Harvey C. Now, my fine fellow—now, Mr. Robert Ffolliott, you said we must meet once again on this side o' the grave, and so we will—ho! ha! (*Conn's head appears over the wall.*) I don't think you'll like this meetin' more than the last. (*Conn, after signing to Robert, gets sitting on the wall, with his legs dangling just above Harvey Duff's head.*) You tould me to have my sowl ready. I wonder if yours is in good condition. Whisht! I hear the boults moving. He is coming! He is—Conn——
(*Conn drops on Harvey Duff's shoulders, who falls forward with a cry—Conn over him. Door opens.* ROBERT *appears.*)
Conn. Run, sir, run! I've got him safe!
(*Robert leaps over Harvey Duff's body, and runs off,* R. *At the same moment Constabulary mount the back wall—leap into Yard. The Sergeant, with a light, appears at the breach in the wall of the Prison.*)
Sergeant. Where is he?
Conn. I've got him—here he is, nivir fear! Hould him fast.
(*The* CONSTABULARY *enter by the door in the wall, and seize Harvey Duff, who is lying on his face.*)
Conn. Don't let him go! Hould him down!
(*Runs off as Constabulary raise Harvey Duff.*)

Kinch. (*Coming round corner,* R.) Where is he?
Harvey Duff! Bungling fools, he has escaped!
(*Harvey Duff gesticulates faintly, and falls back.*)

SCENE VI.—*The Coot's Nest.—Night.*

Robert. (*Entering,* R.) Escaped once more, and free! My disguise is secreted here in some nook of the rocks—in Conn's cupboard, as he calls it—but I cannot find it in the darkness. I hope the poor fellow has got clear away. I would not have him hurt for my sake. (*A whistle.*) Ah! there he is! (*He whistles.*) Thank you, kind Providence, for protecting him. Here he comes—leaping from crag to crag like a goat.

Conn. (*Entering,* R.) Hurroo! tare an' ages, Masther, jewel, but we did that well! But it goes agin my conscience that I did not crack the skull of that thief when I had him fair and asy under my foot. I'll never get absolution for that!

Robert. We must not remain in this place—it is the first they will search. I must make my way to St. Bridget's Abbey at once; there Arte is waiting for me. Where is my great coat, my hat, and beard?

Conn. I have the bundle snug inside. But sure, the Captain knows you in that skin. Didn't he meet you here? It will be no cover for you now. Whisht!

Robert. What! Do you hear anything?

Conn. No; but Tatthers does. I left the baste to watch on the cliff above. There agin; d'ye hear him? 'He's givin' tongue; lie close. I'll go see what it is. [*Exit* L.

Robert. Yonder is the schooner, creeping in with the tide. I can reach the ruins by the seashore; the rocks will conceal me. Then one brief moment with my darling girl——

Re-enter CONN, *with the coat, hat, and beard.*

Conn. Speak low; they are close by.

Robert. The constabulary?

Conn. Yes; and wid them those smugglin' thieves, Mangan, Sullivan, and Reilly; they are gnidin' the polis—the mongrel curs go do that! They know every hole in these rocks.

Robert. But the signal—who will set the match to the tar barrel on Rathgarron Head?

Conn. Nivir fear, sir. Miss Claire is there by this time, and waitin' beside it, lookin' an' listenin' for the two gunshots your honour will fire in the ruins beyant.

Robert. Where is my pistol? (*Feeling in his pocket.*) I cannot find it—gone! No; it cannot be lost. By Heaven! it must have fallen from my pocket as I climbed the wall!
(*Putting on disguise.*)

Conn. Murther alive! what will we do now?

Robert. I must swim out to the schooner.

Conn. It is a mile, an' agin the tide. Stop! will ye lave it to me, and I'll go and I'll find a way of getting them two shots for me? Ah, do, sir! Only this once give me my head an' let me go.

Robert. What do you propose to do?

Conn. Don't you recollect once when the Bally-ragget hounds couldn't find a fox, after dhrawing every cover in the country, damn a hair of one could they smell, an' the whole field lookin' blazes. You were masther of the hunt. "What will we do at all?" says you. "You shall have a fox," ses I, and I whipt in a red herring into the tail o' me coat and away I wint across the fields.

Robert. Ha! ha! I remember it well.

Conn. You, he! an' a devil a one on the whole field but yourself knew that there was a two-legged fox to the fore. Now, I'll give them vagabones another taste of the red herring. I will cut in and cross your scent. I'll lade them off, nivir fear, and be jabers I'll show them the finest run of the huntin' sayson.

Robert. How, Conn, how?

Conn. Asy—look where they are coming down the cliff; slip out this way, quick, before they catch sight of us; when we get round the corner we must divide up; you go by the shore below, I'll take the cliff above. [*Exit Robert,* R.] Begorra, it isn't the first time I've played the fox!
[*Exit,* R.

SCENE VII.—*Rathgarron Head.*

Enter CLAIRE *and* MOLINEUX, L.

Claire. (R.) Here we are at Rathgarron Head—are you not tired?

Mol. I don't know. If you asked if I was dying I should say I could not tell. I feel as if it was all a dream, in which I am not myself.

Claire. Who are you, then?

Mol. Somebody much happier than I can ever be. I wish I could describe to you the change that has taken place in me since we met.

Claire. Oh, I can understand it, for I feel the very——
(*Stops suddenly.*)

Mol. Eh! what do you feel?

Claire. Do you see those ruins on yonder headland? That is St. Bridget's Abbey! A lovely ruin! How effective is that picture, with the moon shining on it!

Mol. Splendid, no doubt; but when I'm beside you I cannot admire ruins or moonshine. The most effective picture is on this headland, and I cannot detach my eyes from the loveliness that is before me.

Claire. (*Aside.*) I cannot stand this. I never played so contemptible a part.

Mol. What is the matter?

Claire. Go home—go away! Why did you come here?

Mol. My dear Miss Ffolliott, I hope I have not been intruding on you. If I have, I pray you forgive me. I will retrace my steps. (*Going.*)

Claire. No, stop!

Mol. (*Returning.*) Yes.

Claire. I encouraged you to follow me.

Mol. I fear I pressed myself upon you.

Claire. (*Aside.*) Oh! why is he so willingly deceived! His gentleness and truth make me ashamed of the part I play. (*Moves to* R.)

Mol. I have said or done something to offend you. Tell me what it is. It will afford me much pleasure to plead for pardon for what I haven't done.

Claire. You want to know what ails me?

Mol. Yes.

Claire. Do you see that tar barrel? (R.)

Mol. Good gracious! what has a tar-barrel got to do with my offence?

Claire. Nothing; but it has everything to do with mine.

Mol. (*Aside, after a pause.*) I wonder whether there's madness in the family?

Claire. Do you see that tar barrel?

Mol. I see something like a tar-barrel in that pile of brushwood.
Claire. Will you oblige me with a match?
Mol. Certainly. (*Aside.*) There's no doubt about it. So lovely, and yet so afflicted! I feel even more tenderly towards her than I did!
Claire. If I were to ask you to light that bonfire, would you do it?
Mol. With pleasure. (*Aside.*) It is the moon that affects her. I wish I had an umbrella.
Claire. Captain Molineux, my brother has escaped from the prison, guarded by your soldiers. He is now in yonder ruins. This pile of fuel, when lighted, will be the signal for the schooner you see yonder to send a boat ashore to take off the fugitive. I have been a decoy to entice you away from your duty, so that I might deprive your men of the orders they await to pursue my brother, who has broken gaol. Now do you understand my conduct?
Mol. Miss Ffolliott!
Claire. Now do you understand why every tender word you have spoken has tortured me like poison? Why every throb in your honest heart has been a knife in mine?
Mol. I thought you were mad. I fear 'tis I have been so.
Claire. You can redeem your professional honour; you can repair the past. I have no means here of lighting that beacon. If the signal is not fired, my brother will be recaptured; but the blood that revolts in my heart against what I am doing is the same that beats in his. He would disdain to owe his liberty to my duplicity and to your infatuation. There's your road. Good night!
[*Claire goes out hastily.—Music.*

Mol. So I have been her dupe! No—she was not laughing at me! (*Looks off.*) She is not laughing at me, as one who—see where she has thrown herself on the ground. I hear her sobs. I cannot leave her alone, and in this wild place; and yet what can I do to—poor thing!—I—I don't know how to act. There again—oh, what a moan that was! I cannot let her lie there!

[*Hastily exit,* R.

SCENE VIII.—*The Ruins of St Bridget's Abbey.*—ARTE *discovered kneeling before the broken shrine,* L.—MOYA *is looking towards* R *down the cliff.*

Moya. There is not a sound to be heard barrin' the sheam of the waves as they lick the shore below.
Arte. I was afraid to come here alone. Even with you beside me I tremble.
Moya. There's something moving in the strand below. Look, miss, it is a goat! (*Arte crosses to* R.) There it is, creeping under the shadow of the rocks.
Arte. I see nothing!
Moya. Whisht! I'll give him the offis.
(*She sings.*)

Enter H. DUFF, REILLY, SULLIVAN, *and* DOYLE. *They carry carbines.* L. 2 E.

Harvey Duff. There they are—there's a pair of them—'tis Moya with her. The constabulary are giving him chase, but here is where he will run to airth—here's the trap, and there's the bait.
Arte. There, there he is! and see those men pursue him! Fly, Robert, fly!
Moya. They will catch him, miss.

Arte. No; he gains upon them—he has turned the point. He will scale the cliff on this side.
(*Crosses to* L. *as if to meet him.*)
Harvey D. (*Seizing Moya.*) Reilly, take hould of her—quick.
(*Reilly seizes Arte—drags her to front of shrine.*)
Arte. Who are you, who dare to lay hands on me? Do you know who I am?
Harvey D. Yes, I do, well enough. You are the sweetheart of the man we want to catch.
Arte. (*Crying.*) Robert! Robert! beware!
Harvey D. Stop her screeching—she'll scare him off (*Sullivan crosses to* R. C.)
Moya. Help! murther! thieves! fire!
Harvey D. Hould your yelp, or I'll choke you—och—gorra—she's bitin' me!
Moya (*Cries.*) Don't come here—don't come.
(*Stifles her cries with the handkerchief he tears from her head.*)
Kinch (*Looking over the parapet,* R.) We have lost his track.
Harvey D. Aye, but we have found it—here he comes—stand close now, an head him off. (*Kinchela disappears,* R. *The figure of Robert Ffolliott is seen emerging from one side of the ruin,* L. *He advances, Sullivan and Doyle both start out. He looks from side to side.*) Stand and surrender! (*He rushes up the ruins to the window at the back.*) Fire, Sullivan—give it to him. Why don't you fire? (*Sullivan fires—the shot takes effect—he falls, and rolls down to a lower platform.*) Ha! ha! that stopped him—he's got it. (*He raises himself, and faintly tries to escape by a breach in the wall,* L.) Give it to them again! (*Doyle fires—He falls, and tumbling from one platform to another, rolls on his face on the stage—Reilly releasing Arte at second shot, gets* L. *of her.*)
Kinch. (*Appearing* R.) What are you about? Those two shots are the signal, and see the fire is lighted on Rathgarron Head.
Harvey D. 'Tis lighted too late!
(*Throws Moya up,* R. C.)
Kinch. No; for there comes the boat from the schooner, and see that man in the water swimming towards her? 'Tis Robert Ffolliott escaped!
Harvey D. Oho! if that's Robert Ffolliott, I'd like to know who's this?
Conn. (*Raising himself slowly, and allowing his hat and beard to fall back, and facing Harvey D., with smile on his blood-stained face*). The Shaughraun!

(*He falls back. Moya, who has been released by Harvey D. in his astonishment, utters a faint cry, and throws herself upon the body. A ray of moonlight striking through the ruined window, falls on the figure of the Saint on the Shrine, whose extended arms seem to invoke protection over the prostrate group*).

ACT III.

SCENE I.—*Mrs. O'Kelley's Cottage.—Music.*

Enter FATHER DOLAN *and* CLAIRE, L.

Father D. Be patient, Claire!
Claire. Patient! My cousin has disappeared—no trace of Arte can be found—Moya has also been spirited away—perhaps murdered, as they murdered Conn!

Father D. (*Knocking at door*). Mrs. O'Kelly, 'tis I—Father Dolan.

Enter MRS. O'KELLY, D. F. R.

Mrs. O'K. (C.) Blessings on your path; it always leads to the poor and to the sore-hearted!
Father D. (R.) This is a sad business! Did you hear why they killed your poor boy?
Mrs. O'K. (*Sobbing*). Because he'd got a fine shute of clothes on him; they shot at the man that wasn't in it, and they killed my poor boy!
Claire (L.). Did they bring him home insensible?
Mrs. O'K. No, miss—they brought him home on a shutter, an' there now he lies wid Tatthers beside him. The cratur' won't let a hand go near the body.
Claire. Poor fellow! he met his death while aiding my brother to escape.

Enter MOLINEUX, L.

You see what your men have done!
Mrs. O'K. It was the polis, not the sodgers, murthered him. Don't blame the Captain, miss; God bless him, he was in my cabin before daylight—he never spoke a word, but he put five goolden pounds in my hand (*Crosses to him.*); and, thanks to himself, my Conn will have the finest wake this day! wid Nancy Malone and Biddy Madigan for keeners—There'll be ating and dhrinking, and six of the O'Kellys to carry him out as grand as a mimber o' parliament—Och hone!—my darlin' boy, it will be a grand day for you, but your poor ould mother will be left alone in her cabin buried alive while yourself is going to glory—och—o—o—hone!
[*Exit*, L., *crying*.
Mol. In the name of Bedlam does she propose to give a dance and a supper party in honour of the melancholy occasion!
Claire. They are only going to wake poor Conn!
Father D. And your five pounds will be spent in whisky, and cakes, and consolation, and fiddlers, and grief, and meat and drink for the poor.
Mol. What a compound! You Irish do mix up your——
Claire. (*Interrupting him.*) Never mind what we mix—have you discovered any traces of Arte and Moya? Have you done anything?
Mol. I've been thinking.
Claire. Thinking! what's the good of thinking? My cousin Arte has been stolen—where is she? The country is full of police and soldiers, and yet two girls have been carried off under your noses—perhaps murdered, for all you know or care—and there you stand like a goose, thinking!
Mol. Pray don't be so impetuous. You Irish——
Claire. I won't be called "You Irish."
Mol. I beg your pardon; you do make me so nervous.
Claire. Oh, do I! My impetuosity didn't make you nervous last night, did it? No matter; go on—a penny for your thoughts.
Mol. If Miss O'Neal and Moya were present in the ruins when Conn was shot, they must have been witnesses of the deed. Since then they have disappeared. It struck me that those who killed the boy must have some reason for removing all evidences of the transaction.
Father D. He is right.
Claire. Well?
Mol. I questioned the constabulary, and find they had no hand in it. The deed was done by a posse of fellows assembled to assist in the pursuit by a police agent named Harvey Duff!
Father D. and Claire. Harvey Duff!
Mol. You know him?
Claire. He has thought it out while we have been blundering. Blinded by our tears, we could not see; deafened by our complaints, we could not hear. (*Seizes both his hands.*) Forgive me!
Mol. There she goes again! I've done nothing to deserve all this.
Claire. Nothing! You have unearthed the fox, you have drawn the badger; now the rogue is in sight our course is clear. (*Crosses to* R.)
Mol. It is? I confess I don't see it!
Father D. These two girls were the only witnesses of the deed!
Claire. And that is why they have been carried off?
Father D. No one else was present to prove how Conn was killed.
Conn. (*Looking out of the window,* F. L.) Yes; I was there!
All. Conn alive!
Conn. Whisht! No; I'm dead!
Father D. Why, you provoking vagabond—(*Up to him*)—is this the way you play upon our feelings? Are you hurt?
Conn. I've a crack over the lug, an' a scratch across the small o' me back. Sure, miss, if I hadn't dhrawed them to shoot, you'd have never had the signal.
Mol. Brave fellow! how did you escape?
Conn. I'll tell you, sir; but—whoo! gorra!—dead men tell no tales, an' here I am takin' away the character of the corporation. When the masther got out of jail, there was Kinchela an' his gang waitin' outside to murdther us. We ga' them the slip; and while the masther got off, I led them away afther me to St. Bridget's. Then, afther I got them two shots out of them, I rouled down an' lay as quiet as a sack of pitaties.
Claire. Arte and Moya were in the ruins?
(*Goes to him.*)
Conn. They were standing by and thrying to screech blue murther. "Stop their mouths," said a voice that I knew was Kinchela's. Sullivan and Reilly whipt them up and put them on a car that was waitin' outside. After that, sorra a thing I remember till I found myself laid out on a shutter, wid candles all around me, an' whisky bottles, an' cakes, an' sugar, an' lemon, an' tobacco, an' bacon, an' snuff, an' the devil in all! I thought I was in heaven.
Father D. And that's his idea of heaven you dead?—and you let your poor ould mother believe you dead?—you did not relieve her sorrow?
Conn. Would you have me spile a wake afther invitin' all the neighbours?
Mol. Will you allow me on this occasion to say, "You Irish——"
Claire. Yes, and you need not say any more.
Conn. Then I remembered the polis would be wanting me for the share I had in helping the masther to break jail. Ah, sir, don't let on to the mother—she'd never hould her whisht; an' I want to be dead, if you please, to folly up the blackguards that have hoult of Moya and Miss O'Neal.
Mol. Do you know the place where these ruffians resort?
Conn. I'm conceited I do.
Father D. I'll answer for him; he knows every disreputable den in the country.

Conn. What would you do now, if I didn't?
Claire. Here comes your mother with the mourners.
Conn. Hoo! she'll find some of the whisky gone.
(*Disappears.*)
Claire. Now what's to be done?
Mol. I will proceed at once to Ballyragget House, and see Mr. Kinchela. I will confront him with this evidence.
Claire. You don't know him.
Mol. I think I do; but he does not know me.
Claire. You will fight him.
Mol. Oh, no. I looked in his eye; there's no fight there; men who bully women have the courage of the cur—there's no pluck in them. I shall take a guard and arrest him for aiding your brother to escape, that he might murder him safely during his flight.
Claire. Who can prove it.

Enter ROBERT, L.
Robert. I can!
Claire. Robert!
(*Crosses to him—embrace.*)
Father D. (R.) Good gracious, what brings you back?
Robert. The news I heard on board the schooner. A pardon has been granted to the Fenian prisoners.
Claire. A pardon?
Mol. I congratulate you, sir. (*Shakes hands with Robert.—Robert and Claire crosses to* R. C.) Oh, by Jove! Excuse my swearing, but a light breaks in upon me—Kinchela knew of this pardon. I'll go to Ballyragget House at once.
Robert. I have just come from there. I went to tax him with his villainy. He has fled.
Mol. I thought there was no fight in him.
Claire. But Arte is in his power.
Robert. Arte in his power! what do you mean?
Claire. He loves her—he has carried her off.
Robert. My wife and her fortune. Ha! he played for a high game.
Mol. And on finding he could not win, he stole half the stakes.
Father D. This man is in league with a desperate crew, half ruffians, half smugglers. Their dens, known only to themselves, are in the bogs and caves of the sea-shore.
Robert. I'll unearth him wherever he is. (*Music.*) I'll hunt him with every honest lad of the county Sligo in the pack, and kill him like a rat.
(*Crosses to* R.)
Mol. I'll send over to Sligo, and get a warrant to arrest this fellow. I like to have the law on my side. If we are to have a hunt, let us have a license. Where shall I find you?
Father D. At my house.
Claire. (*To Robert, who offers his arm to her.*) No, give your arm to Father Dolan.
Father D. Free, and at home! Heaven be praised!
Robert. Not free till Arte is so.
[*Exit with Father D.,* R.
Claire. (*After watching them off, turns and advances rapidly to Molineux.*) What's your Christian name, or have you English such things amongst you?
Mol. Yes, my Christian name is Harry!
Claire. Harry!
[*Kissing him. She runs off,* R. *He assumes a military position and marches off,* R., *whistling "The British Grenadiers."*

Voices. (*Outside,* L.) Oh! Ohone! Oh, hould up. Don't give way.

Enter MRS. O'KELLY, NANCY MALONE, BIDDY MADIGAN, *and* PEASANTS, L. DOYLE *and* WOMEN, *six or seven* MEN, *one* WOMAN. *They exeunt at once,* D. F.

Mrs. O'K. You are kindly welcome. The dark cloud is over the house, but——
Nancy. We come to share the sorrow that's in it this hour.
Biddy. It will be a fine berrin', Mrs. O'Kelly. There will be a grand waste of victuals.
Mrs. O'K. Step inside, ma'am.
(*They all enter the cabin. A woman enters* L., *and exits (cottage.) Then Reilly, followed by Sullivan.—Music. The voices of the Keeners are heard inside singing an Irish lament. During this, other Peasants and Girls enter in couples, and go into cabin.—Scene changes.*)

SCENE II.—*Mrs. O'Kelly's Cabin (Interior.) Door in* F. R., *Fireplace* R. *Conn is lying on a shutter,* L., *supported by an old table, a three-legged stool, and a keg, Table* E., *covered with food and drinking cups, plates of snuff, jugs of punch, lighted candles in bottles, &c.—Tableau of an Irish Wake. A group of women around Conn,* L. C. MRS. O'K. *seated* R.C. MRS. MALONE *and* REILLY *near her, seated* R. SULLIVAN, DOYLE, *and Peasantry (male and female) at table,* R. *The women (seated) are rocking to and fro during the wail.*

CHORUS.—"*The Oolaghaun.*"

Male voices—
Och, Oolaghaun!—och, Oolaghaun!
Make his bed both wide and deep!
Och, Oolaghaun!—och, Oolaghaun!
He's only gone to sleep!

Female voices—
Why did ye die?—oh, why did ye die?
And lave us all alone to cry?

Together—
Why did ye die?—why did ye die?
Laving us to sigh, och hone!
Why did ye die?—why did ye die?
Oolaghaun!—oh, Oolaghaun!

(*During the following rhapsody the music of the wail and the chorus subdued recurs as if to animate the Keeners*).

Biddy. Oh, oh, oho! (*Rocking herself*). Oh, oo, Oolaghaun! The widdy had a son—an only son—wail for the widdy!
Chorus. (*All*)—
Why did ye die?—why did ye die?
Biddy. I see her when she was a fair young girl —a fine girl, wid a child at her breast.
Chorus—
Laving us to sigh! Och, hone!
Biddy. Then I see a proud woman wid a boy by

by her side. He was as bould as a bull-calf that runs beside of the cow.

Chorus—
Why did ye die?—why did ye die?

Biddy. For the girl grew ould as the child grew big, and the woman grew wake as the boy grew strong. (*Rising, and flinging back her hair*). The boy grew strong, for she fed him wid her heart's blood. Ah, hogoola! where is he now? Cowld in his bed! Why did ye die? (*Sits.*)

Chorus—
Laving us to sigh! Och, hone!

(*All the women on the L. join crowd up stage,* R. C.)

Biddy. None was like him—none could compare, and——Good luck to ye, gi' me a dhrop of something to put the sperret in one, for the fire's getting low.

(*Sullivan hands her his jug of punch.*)

Mrs. O'K. Oh, oh! its mighty consolin' to hear this. Mrs. Malone, you are not ating.

Nancy No, ma'am, I'm drinkin'. I dhrink now and agin by way of variety. Biddy is not up to herself.

Reilly. Oh! wait till she'll rise on the top of a noggin.

Biddy. (*After drinking places the jug beside her,* L, *and rises on low stool.*) He was brave! he was brave! he was open-handed! he had the heart of a lion, and the legs of a fox.

(*Conn takes the jug, empties it quietly, and, unobserved by all, replaces it on stool.*)

Biddy. His voice was softer than the cuckoo of an evening, and sweeter than the blackbird afther a summer shower. Ye colleens, ye will nivir hear the voice of Conn again.

(*Sits and blows her nose.*)

Conn. (*Aside.*) It's a mighty pleasant thing to die like this, once in a way, and hear all the good things said about ye afther you're dead and gone, when they can do you no good.

Biddy. His name will be the pride of the O'Kellys for evermore.

Conn. (*Aside.*) I was a big blackguard when I was alive.

Biddy. Noble and beautiful!

Conn. (*Aside.*) Ah! go on out o' that!

Biddy. (*Taking up her jug.*) Oh, he was sweet and sthrong —— Who the devil's been at my jug of punch?

(*Goes up to crowd.*)

Mrs. O'K. (*Sobbing and rising.*) Nobody is dhrinkin'—yez all despise the occasion—if yez lave behind ye liquor enough to swim a fly—oh, hoo! There's a hole in your mug, Mr. Donovan, I'd be glad to see it in the bottle—oh, hoo!

(*Knock without,* R. D.)

Sullivan. What's that?

(*The door is opened.*)

Enter MOLINEUX.—*They all rise.*

Mol. I don't come to disturb this—a—melancholy—a—entertainment—I mean a—this festive solemnity——

Mrs. O'K. (*Wiping own chair for him with her apron.*) Heaven bless you for coming to admire the last of him. Here he is—ain't he beautiful? (*Leads him up.*)

Mol. (*Aside.*) The vagabond is winking at me.

I've great mind to kick the keg from under him and send him reeling on the floor.

(*Sullivan offers him snuff,* R.)

Mrs. O'K. How often have I put him to bed as a child, and sung him to sleep! . Now he will be put to bed with a shovel, and oh! the song was nivir sung that will awaken him.

Mol. If any words could put life into him, I came here to speak them. (*Music.*) Robert Ffolliott has been pardoned and has returned home a free man.

All. Hurroo! hurroo!

Mol. But his home is desolate, for the girl he loves has been stolen away. The man who robbed him of his liberty first, then his estate, has now stolen his betrothed.

All. Who is it?

Mol. Mr. Corry Kinchela. The ruffians who shot that brave fellow who lies there were led by Kinchela's agent, Harvey Duff.

All. Harvey Duff!

(*Biddy seizes axe from* L.—*Mrs. O. K. crosses to fire for poker.—Donovan gets scythe and kneels* R, *sharpening it with stone.—Tableaux.*)

(*Molineux first encounters the edge of axe—stepping back, confronts Mrs. K. with the poker — which she flourishes savagely—and, crossing in front, eyes with his glass Donovan sharpening scythe.*)

Biddy. Harvey Duff sent my only boy across the say?

Donovan. I've a long reckoning agin him; but I've kept it warm in my heart.

Mrs. O'K. An' I've a short one, and there it lies!

(*Pointing to Conn.*)

All. Where is he?

Mol. Kinchela and his men are hiding in some den, where they hold Miss O'Neal and Moya prisoners.

All. Moya Dolan?

Mol. The niece of your minister!—the sweetheart of poor Conn! My men shall aid you in the search; but you are familiar with every hole and corner in the county—you must direct it. Robert Ffolliott awaits you all at Suil-a-beg to lead the hunt—that is, after you have paid your melancholy respects to the Shaughraun.

Mrs. O'K. No; you could not plaze him better than to go now. Bring back the news that you have revenged his murder, an' he'll go under the sod wid a light heart.

All. Hurroo! To Suil-a-beg!—To Suil-a-beg!

[*Exeunt rapidly, All,* R. D. *but Reilly and Sullivan. Molineux gives Conn a pinch of snuff — he sneezes.— Reilly and Sullivan turn and watch him off; then rush down* C.

Reilly. (R. C.) Sullivan, you must warn Kinchela. Quick! There's not an hour to lose.

Sullivan. (L. C.) Where shall I find him?

(*Conn rises and listens.*)

Reilly. At the Coot's Nest! The lugger came in last night. Tell him to get aboord—take the two women wid him, for he'll have to run for his life.

Sullivan. Ay, and, bedad, for ours too! If he's caught we're in for it.

(*Conn creeps to door, and locks it very quietly.*)

Reilly. I feel the rope around my neck.

(*Going* R.)

Sullivan. The other end is chokin' me.
(*Going* L.)
(*As they turn to go they face Conn, they stagger back astonished.*)
Both. Murdher, alive!
Conn. That's what I am. Murdher, alive! that will live to see you both hanged for it. (*Advances.*) I'll be at your wake, and begorra I'll give you both a fine charaoter. (*Sullivan and Reilly rush to the door.*) Asy, boys, asy! The dure is fast an' here's the key. You're in a fine thrap, ho! ho! Yez made a mistake last night. (*Sullivan whispers Reilly.*) Take it asy now.
(*They rush to the tables* R., *and each seizes a knife.*)
Reilly. (R.) Did ye forget ma bouchal that ye're dead?
Sullivan.. (*Advancing slowly,* L.) Sure, if we made a mistake last night—we can repair it now!
Conn. Oh—tare an' ages—what'll I do?
(*Retreats behind table,* R.)
Reilly. We'll just lay you out agin comfortable where you wor. Devil a sowl will be the wiser.
Conn. Help! help!
(*Reilly advances and receives the contents of a mug; then Sullivan, who gets the plate of snuff in his eyes. Conn jumps over the table, and makes for the window at back.*)
Reilly. Screeching won't save ye! They are miles away by this time.
Conn. (*Rushing to window, and dashing the shutters open.*) Help!
(*Reilly and Sullivan drag Conn back by the hair of his head, and throw him down.*)
Sullivan. Shut the windy! I'll quiet him!

MOLINEUX *appears at window.*

Mol. (*Presenting revolver.*) Drop those knives! (*A pause.*) Do you hear what I said—drop those knives! (*They let their knives fall.*) Now open the door!
Conn. There's the key! (*Hands it to Reilly.*) *Reilly doggedly unlocks the door.* MOLINEUX *appears at door and enters.*) Help me up! (*To* *Sullivan.*) The hangman will do as much for you, one day.

(*Sullivan helps Conn to rise.*)

Mol. (R. C.) Now! (*Reilly makes a start as if he would escape.*) If you put your head outside the cabin, I'll put a bullet in it! (*Reilly retires down stage,* R.) What men are these?
Conn. (L. C.) Two of Kinchela's chickens. They know the road we want to thraval.
Mol. Take that! (*Hands Conn the revolver.*) Do you know how to use it?
Conn. I'll thry! (*Turns to Sullivan.*) What part of the world would like to be sent to?
(*Pointing weapon at him.*)
Mol. (*Drawing his sword and turning to Reilly.*) Attention, my friend! Now put your hands in your pockets! (*Repeats.—Reilly obeys him.*) Now take me direct to where your employer, Mr. Kinchela, has imprisoned Miss O'Neal; and if, on the road, you take your hands out of your pockets, and attempt to move beyond the reach of my sword, upon my honour, as an officer and a gentleman, I shall cut you down! Forward!
[*Exeunt,* D. F. R.

Conn. Attintion! Put your hand in my pocket. (*Sullivan obeys him.*) Now take me straight to where Moya Dolan is shut up; an' if ye stir a peg out o' that on the road, by the piper that played before Julius Cæsar, I'll save the country six feet of rope.
(*As they go out scene changes.*)

SCENE III.—*Hogan's Shanty.* (*Lights half down.*)

Enter ARTE *and* MOYA, L.

Arte. 'Tis getting dark. Will they keep us another night in this fearful place?
Moya. I don't care what becomes of me. I wish they would kill me, as they killed Conn—I've nothin' to live for!
Arte. I have! I'll live to bring Kinchela to the dock, where he brought my Robert. I'll live to tear the mask from his face!
(*Crosses to* L.)
Moya. I'd like to put my ten commandments on the face of. Harvey Duff—the murdherin' villain, if I should only live to see him go up a ladder, and spoil a market.

Enter KINCHELA, D. F. L.

Kinch. (*Crossing to Arte.*) You look pale; but I see you kape a proud lip still, Miss O'Neal. You despise me now, but afther another month or two, never fear, we'll get on finely together.
Arte. Do you dream you can keep up here for a month? Why, before a week has passed there's not a sod in the county (*crosses to* C.) Sligo but will be turned up to search for us, and then we'll see who'll look the paler, you or I.
Kinch. Before midnight you will be safe on board a lugger that lies snug beside this shanty, and before daylight you and I will be on our way to a delightful rotirement, where you and I will pass our honeymoon together.
Moya. And what's to become of me?
(*Music.*)

Enter HARVEY DUFF, *with* MANGAN *and* DOYLE, R.

Harvey D. I'll take care of you! The wind is fair, and the tide will serve in an hour. Come, ladies, all on board is the word, if you plaze.
(*Mangan and Doyle seize Arte and Moya.*)
Arte. Kinchela, I implore you not to add this cowardly act to your list of crimes! Release me and this girl, and, on my honour, I will bear no witness against you, nor against any concerned in last night's work.
Kinch. It is too late.
Arte. (*Struggling with Doyle.*) Kinchela, if you have any respect—any love for me, will you see me outraged thus?
Harvey D. (*Aside to Kinch.*) Ffolliott has returned.
Kinch. Ha! (*Crosses to* R.) Away with them!
Moya. (*To Mangan.*) Lave your hould, I'll go asy!
(*Drops her cloak while struggling with Mangan, she releases herself and boxes his ears. Arte is taken off first by Doyle* R.)
Harvey D. (L.) Robert Ffolliott is pardoned, and he's huntin' the bogs this minute, with half the county Sligo at his back.
Kinch. Never fear, they can't discover this place till we are gone. No one ever knew of it but our own fellows.

Harvey D. And Conn, the Shanghraun.
Kinch. He is wiped out.
Harvey D. We are safe.
Kinch. Go, keep watch on the cliff (*crosses to* L.) while I get these girls aboard.
Harvey D. I'll be onaisy in my mind till we are clear o' this. [*Exit,* R.
Kinch. Robert Ffolliott pardoned, afther all the throuble I took to get him convicted? And this is the way a loyal man is thrated! I am betrayed. No matther; if he can recover his estate, he can't recover his wife. She is mine—mine! She hates me now, but I concait she'll get over that. [*Exit* R.

Enter CONN *and* SULLIVAN, D. F. L.

Conn. Not a sowl in it—you deceive me!
Sullivan. No, they are here! (*Points to the cloak.*) What's that?
Conn. Moya's cloak! (*He picks it up. Releases Sullivan, who creeps off while Conn examines cloak.*) 'Tis hers—she's here! Oh, he's slipped out of my pocket—he's off—gone to rouse up the whole pack! What'll I do? Where can I hide until the masther an' the Captain come up? They can't be far behind. If I could get behind one of them big hogsheads, or inside one o' them. Whisht! there was a cry. 'Twas Miss O'Neal's voice. I am only one agin twenty, but I'll make it lively for them while it lasts! [*Exit* R.

SCENE IV.—*Shed looking out upon a Rocky Cave*) *The topmasts of a ship are seen over the edge of the precipice. Bales, kegs, hogsheads, naval gear lie about* R. *and* L.—*Music.—Break of day.*

Enter HARVEY DUFF *rapidly,* 1 E. R. *He looks round, and he is very pale.*

Harvey D. Kinchela, hurry—quick!

Enter KINCHELA, L.

Kinch. What's the matter?
Harvey D. I was watching on the cliff above, where I could hear the shouts of the people in the glen as they hunted every hole in the rocks. I could see Robert Ffolliott and Miss Claire hounding them on; when I turned my eyes down here, and on this very place where we are standing I saw——
Kinch. Who?
Harvey D. Conn, the Shaughraun!
Kinch. You are mad with fright. (*Up the rock.*)
Harvey D. So wonld you be, if you saw a dead man as plain as I saw him. (*Distant cries and shouts.*) D'ye hear them?—they are coming close to us!
Kinch. Go back to your post on the cliff, and keep watch while I get these women on board. We have no time to lose. Mangan! Doyle!
Harvey D. (*Who has been looking round.*) I'll be on my oath I saw him here! [*Exit,* R.

Enter MOYA *and* MANGAN, 1 E. L.

Moya. Where do you want me to go?
Kinch. On board that ship below there.
Moya. Do you think I'm a fly, or a seagull? (*Down to corner,* L.)
Kinch. You see this ladder?—by that road you can gain the ledge below. There we'll find a basket—we'll send you down like a bucket in a well.
Moya. If I don't choose to go down?
Kinch. Then you'll be carried, my beauty!
Moya. Stand off!
Kinch. Tie her hands. Mangan, go get me a taste of rope!
[*He seizes her. Mangan exits,* 2. E. L.
Moya. Help! help! Is there nivir a man within reach of my voice?
Kinch. Mangan, bring the rope, curse you!
Moya. Help! murdher! fire!
(*A shot is fired from the hogshead,* R. *Kinchela throws up his hands—staggers, falls,* L. C. *Moya utters a cry, and falls on her knees,* R., *and covering her face with her hands. The hogshead rises a little—advances to Moya, and covers her like an extinguisher. The legs of Conn have been seen under the barrel as it moves. Enter* MANGAN, 2 E. L., *with the rope.* DOYLE *with* ARTE, 1 E. L. SULLIVAN, 2 E. L. *Sullivan kneels over Kinchela.*)

Mangan. Who fired that shot?
Doyle. She has killed him, and escaped!
Arte. Brave girl! she has avenged me.
Sullivan. He's not dead. See, he moves! There's life in him still. (*Shouts outside.*)
Doyle. They are coming!—away wid ye to the lugger. Quick!
(*The men look off,* R.)
Sullivan. Must we lave him here?
(*Crosses to corner,* R.)
Doyle. We can't carry him down the ladder.
(*During the foregoing Arte creeps to the back.*)
Sullivan. Everyone for himself; the devil take the hindmost. (*Going up to rock piece.*)
Arte. (*Who has lifted the end of the ladder.*) Stop where you are! (*Throws the ladder over.*) I have been your prisoner; now you are mine!

(*Shouts outside nearer.*)
(*The men look bewildered from side to side, and then rush off,* 1 E. L. *Conn pops his head out from the top of the hogshead, and looks out.*)

Conn. Is that you, miss?
Arte. Conn, where's Moya?
Conn. She's inside. (*Shouts.*)
(*Conn disappears, raises the hogshead. They emerge from it.*)
Harvey D. (*Outside.*) Kinchela, away wid you—quick!
Conn. Stand aside. Here comes the flower of the flock. (*Shouts.*)
(*They retire—Arte to* L., *behind shed; Conn and Moya to* R.)

HARVEY DUFF *rushes on from* 1 E. R., *very pale.*

Harvey D. The crowd are upon us; we are betrayed! What's the matter, man? Up, I tell you! Are you mad or drunk? Stop, then; I'm off. (*Runs up to the back.*) The ladder gone!—gone! (*Runs to Kinchela.*) Sphake, man! What will we do?—what does it mean?

ARTE *appears*, L, MOYA, R, *from behind hogshead.*

Moya. It means that the wind has changed and the tide doesn't serve.

Arte. It means that you are on your way to a delightful retirement, where you and he will pass your honeymoon together.

Harvey D. (*Conn advances to his side,* R.) The murdher's out.

Conn. And you are in for it. (*Shouts outside.*) D'ye hear them cries—the hounds are on your track, Harvey Duff!

Harvey D. (L.) What will I do? What will I do?

Conn. Say your prayers, if ever you knew any—for your time is come. Look! There they come—down the cliff side. Ha! they've caught sight of you.

(*Shouts.— Harvey Duff rushes up to the edge of the precipice, looks over, wrings his hands in terror.*)

Conn. D'ye see that wild ould woman, wid the knife? that's Bridget Madigan, whose son's life you swore away.

Harvey D. Save me!—you can—they will tear me into rags. (*To Arte, on his knees.*)

Conn. D'ye know Andy Donovan? that's him with the scythe! You sent his brother across the say! (*Shouts outside.*) Egorra, he knows you! Look at him!

Harvey D. (*On his knees, to Conn.*) Spare me! ity me!

p *Conn.* Ay, as you spared me!—as you spared them at whose side you knelt before the altar!—as you pitied them whose salt you ate, but whose blood you dhrank! There's death coming down upon you from above!—there's death waiting for you below! Now, *informer,* take your choice!

(*Shouts.—Harvey Duff, bewildered with fright, and running alternately to the edge of the cliff and back to look at the approaching crowd, staggers like a drunken man, uttering inarticulate cries of fear.*)

(*The crowd, headed by BIDDY MADIGAN, NANCY MALONE, rush in at 1st and 2nd* E. R. *Uttering a scream of terror, Harvey Duff leaps over the cliff. The crowd pursue him to the edge and lean over.*)

Enter ROBERT FFOLLIOTT, CLAIRE, FATHER DOLAN, *and* CONSTABULARY, R.—Enter MOLINEUX, *followed by* SERGEANT *and* SIX SOLDIERS, *with* MANGAN, SULLIVAN, *and* DOYLE *in custody,* 2 E. L.

Robert (L. *Embracing Arte.*) Arte!

Claire. Has the villain escaped?

Mol. I've bagged a few; but I've missed the principal offender.

Conn. I didn't—there's my bird.

Father D. Is he dead?

(*Molineux approaches Kinchela, and examines him.*)

Mol. I fear not; the bullet has entered here, but it has struck something in his breast. (*Draws out a pocket-book.*) This pocket-book has saved his life!

(*He hands it to Father Dolan, who opens it, draws out letter, and reads.*)

Kinch. (*Reviving and rising.*) Where am I?

Mol. You are in custody.

Kinch. What for?

Mol. For an attempt to assassinate this gentleman!

Kinch. He was a felon, escaping from justice!

Father D. (R. C.) He was a free man, and you knew it, as this letter proves!

(*The crowd utter a cry of rage, and advance towards Kinchela. Father Dolan stands between them and him. Kinchela flies for protection to the constabulary,* R.)

Kinch. Save me—protect me!

Father D. (*Facing the crowd.*). Stand back!—do you hear me. Must I speak twice?

(*The crowd retire, and lower their weapons.*)

Mol. Take him away! (*Crosses to Claire.*)

Kinch. Yes, take me away, quick— don't you hear? or them divils won't give you the chance.

[*Exit with constabulary,* R. 2 E.

Mrs. O'K. (*Outside,* R. 1 E.) Where's my boy? Where is he?

Conn. Och, murdher—here's the ould mother! Hide me!

Enter MRS. O'KELLY.

Mrs. O'K. Where is he—where is my vagabone? (*Father D. brings him forward by the ear.*) Oh, Conn, ye thief o' the world—my boy—my darlin'!

(*Falls on his neck.*)

Conn. Whisht, mother, don't cry. See this—I'll never be kilt again.

Moya. (R. C.) Sure, if he hadn't have been murdhered, he couldn't have saved us.

Mrs. O'K. And after letting me throw all the money away over the wake!

(*Goes up with Conn and Moya.*)

Mol. Turn the ceremony into a wedding. I really don't see you Irish make much distinction.

Claire. (R.) I believe that in England the wedding often turns out the more melancholy occasion of the two.

Mol. (R. C.) Will you try?

Robert. He has earned you, Claire. I give my consent.

Arte. But what is to become of Conn. Father Dolan will never give his consent.

Father D. (*To Conn.*) Come here. Will you reform?

Conn. I don't know what that is, but I will!

Father D. Will you mend your ways, and your coat? No; you can't! How do I know but that you will go poaching of a night?

Conn. Moya will go bail I won't.

Father D. And the drink?

Moya. I will take care there is no hole in the thimble.

Father D. I won't trust either of you—you have deceived me so often. Can you find anyone to answer for you?

Conn. Oh, murdher! What'll I do? Divil a friend I have in the world, barrin Tatthers! (*Moya whispers in his ear.*) Oh! they won't!

Moya. Thry!

Conn. (*To the audience.*) She says you will go bail for me.
Moya. I didn't!
Conn. You did!
Moya. I didn't!

Conn. You are the only friend I have. Long life t'ye!—Many a time have you looked over my faults—will you be blind to them now, and hould out your hands once more to a poor Shaughraun?
Omnes. Hurroo! Hurroo! (*Till curtain.*)

Disposition of the Characters at the Fall of the Curtain.

PEASANTS. PEASANTS. BIDDY. SOLDIERS.
MANGAN.
REILLY.
SULLIVAN.
DOYLE.
SERGEANT.
CLAIRE. MOL. MRS. O'K. MOYA. CONN. FATHER D. ROBERT. ARTE.
R. L.

NOW READY, PRICE ONE SHILLING, PER POST 3d. EXTRA.

ENTRANCES AND EXITS.

BY MRS. E. WINSTANLEY.

A Pathetic Story of Theatrical Life, with Graphic Descriptions of the Trails and Vicissitudes of a Struggling Actor.

BEING No. 8 OF DICKS' ENGLISH NOVELS;

JOHN DICKS, 313, Strand.

ADVERTISEMENTS.

Now Publishing, Price One Penny, Weekly,

DICKS' STANDARD PLAYS,
AND
FREE ACTING DRAMA.
FOR THE REPRESENTATION OF WHICH THERE IS NO LEGAL CHARGE.

1 Othello
2 School for Scandal
3 Werner
4 She Stoops to Conquer
5 The Gamester
6 King Lear
7 New way to Pay old Debts
8 Road to Ruin
9 Merry wives of Windsor
10 The Iron Chest
11 Hamlet
12 The Stranger
13 Merchant of Venice
14 The Honeymoon
15 Pizarro
16 Man of the World
17 Much Ado about Nothing
18 The Rivals
19 Damon and Pythias
20 Macbeth
21 John Bull
22 Fazio
23 Speed the Plough
24 Jane Shore
25 Evadne
26 Antony and Cleopatra
27 The Wonder
28 The miller and his men
29 The Jealous Wife
30 Therese
31 Brutus
32 The Maid of Honour
33 A Winter's Tale
34 The Poor Gentleman
35 The Castle Spectre
36 The Heir-at-Law
37 Love in a Village
38 A Tale of mystery
39 Douglas
40 The Critic
41 George Barnwell
42 Grecian Daughter
43 As You Like It
44 Cato
45 The Beggars' Opera
46 Isabella
47 The Revenge
48 Lord of the Manor
49 Romeo and Juliet
50 Sardanapalus
51 The Hypocrite
52 Venice Preserved
53 The Provoked Husband
54 Clandestine marriage
55 Fair Penitent
56 Two Gentlemen of Verona
57 Fatal Curiosity
58 Belle's Stratagem
59 Manfred
60 Rule a Wife, &c.
61 Bertram
62 Wheel of Fortune
63 The Duke of Milan
64 Good-Natured Man
65 King John
66 Beaux' Stratagem
67 Arden of Faversham
68 Trip to Scarborough
69 Lady Jane Grey
70 Rob Roy
71 Roman Father
72 The Provoked wife
73 The Two Foscari
74 Foundling of the Forest
75 All the World's a Stage
76 Richard III
77 Bold Stroke for a wife
78 Castle of Sorrento
79 The Inconstant
80 Guy Mannering
81 The Busy-Body
82 Tom and Jerry
83 Alexander the Great
84 The Liar

85 The Brothers
86 Way of the world
87 Cymbeline
88 She Would,, &c:
89 Deserted Daughter
90 Wives as They Were, and maids as They Are
91 Every man in his humour
92 Midsummer Night's Dream
93 Tamerlane
94 Bold Stroke for a husband
95 Julius Cæsar
96 All for Love
97 The Tempest
98 Richard Cœur de Lion
99 The Mourning Bride
100 The bashful man
101 Barbarossa
102 The Curfew
103 Merchant of Bruges
104 Giovanni in London
105 Timon of Athens
106 Honest Thieves
107 West Indian
108 The Earl of Essex
109 The Irish Widow
110 The Farmer's Wife
111 Tancred and Sigismunda
112 The Panel
113 Deformed Transformed
114 The Soldier's Daughter
115 Monsieur Tonson
116 The Black Prince
117 School for Wives
118 Coriolanus
119 The Citizen
120 The First Floor
121 The Foundling
122 Oroonoko
123 Love a-la-Mode
124 Richard II
125 Siege of Belgrade
126 Samson Agonistes
127 Maid of the mill
128 One o'Clock
129 Who's the Dupe?
130 Mahomet
131 Duplicity
132 The Devil to Pay
133 Troilus and Cressida
134 Ways and means
135 All in the Wrong
136 Cross Purposes
137 The Orphan
138 Bon Ton
139 Tender Husband
140 El Hyder
141 The Country Girl
142 Midas
143 Castle of Andalusia
144 Two Strings to your Bow
145 Measure for measure
146 The miser
147 Haunted Tower
148 The Tailors
149 Love for Love
150 Robbers of Calabria
151 Zara
152 High Life Below Stairs
153 Marino Faliero
154 The Waterman
155 Vespers of Palermo
156 The Farm-house
157 Comedy of Errors
158 The Romp
159 Distressed mother
160 Atonement [ringe
161 Three Weeks after Mar-
162 Suspicious Husband
163 Dog of Montargis
164 The Heiress
165 The Deserter
166 King Henry VIII
167 Comus

168 Recruiting Sergeant
169 Animal magnetism
170 The Confederacy
171 The Carmelite
172 The Chances
173 Follies of a Day
174 Titus Andronicus
175 Paul and Virginia
176 Know your own mind
177 The Padlock
178 Constant Couple
179 Better Late than Never
180 My Spouse and I
181 Every One has his Fault
182 The Deuce is in him
183 Adopted Child
184 Love rs' Vows
185 Maid of the Oaks
186 The Dnenna
187 Turnpike Gate
188 Lady of Lyons
189 Miss in her Teens
190 Twelfth Night
191 Lodoiska
192 Earl of Warwick
193 Fortune's Frolics
194 Way to keep him
195 Braganza
196 No Song no Supper
197 Taming of the Shrew
198 Spanish Student
199 Double Dealer
200 Mock Doctor
201 Fashionable lover
202 The Guardian
203 Cain
204 Rosina
205 Love's Labour Lost
206 The Hunchback
207 The Apprentice
208 Raising the Wind
209 Lovers' Quarrels
210 Rent Day
211 Cronobotonthologos
212 His first champagne
213 Pericles
214 Robinson Crusoe
215 He's much to Blame
216 Ella Rosenberg
217 The Quaker
218 School of Reform
219 King Henry IV (1)
220 Fifteen Years of a Drunkard's Life
221 Thomas and Sally
222 Bombastes Furioso
223 First Love
224 Somnambulist
225 All's Well that Ends Well
226 Lottery Ticket
227 Gustavus Vasa
228 Sweethearts and Wives
229 Miller of Mansfield
230 Black-Eyed Susan
231 King Henry IV (2)
232 The Station-House
233 Recruiting Officer
234 The Tower of Nesle
235 King Henry V
236 The Rendezvous
237 Appearance is Against Them
238 William Tell
239 Tom Thumb
240 The Rake's Progress
241 King Henry VI (1.)
242 Blue Devils
243 Cheats of Scapin
244 Charles the Second
245 Love makes the man
246 Virginius
247 School for Arrogance
248 The Two Gregories
249 King Henry VI. (2)

250 Mrs. Wiggins
251 Mysterious husband
252 Heart of Midlothian
253 King Henry VI. (3)
254 Illustrious Stranger
255 Register Office
256 Dominique
257 Chapter of Accidents
258 Descarte
259 Hero and Leander
260 Cure for Heartache
261 Siege of Damascus
262 The Secret
263 Deaf and Dumb
264 Banks of the Hudson
265 The Wedding Day
266 Laugh when you can
267 What Next?
268 Raymond and Agnes
269 Lionel and Clarissa
270 Red crow
271 The Contrivance
272 Broken Sword
273 Polly Honeycomb
274 Nell Gwynne
275 Cymon
276 Perfection
277 Count of Narbonne
278 Of Age To-morrow
279 Orphan of China
280 Pedlar's Acre
281 Mogul's Tale
282 Othello Travestie
283 Law of Lombardy
284 Day after the wedding
285 The Jew
286 Irish Tutor
287 Such Things Are
288 The Wife
289 Dragon of Wantley
290 Suil Dhuv
291 Lying Valet
292 Lily of St. Leonards
293 Oliver Twist
294 The Housekeeper
295 Child of Nature
296 Home, Sweet Home
297 Which is the man?
298 Caius Gracchus
299 Mayor of Garratt
300 Woodman
301 Midnight our
302 Woman's Wit
303 The Purse
304 Votary of Wealth
305 Life Buoy
306 Wild Oats
307 Rookwood
308 Gambler's Fate
309 Herne the Hunter
310 "Yes!" and "No!"
311 The Sea-captain
312 Eugene Aram
313 Wrecker's Daughter
314 Alfred the Great
315 { Virginia mummy / Intrigue
316 { My Neighbour's wife / Married Bachelor
317 Richelieu
318 Money
319 Ior.
320 The Bridal
321 Paul Pry
322 Love-chase
323 Glencoe
324 { Spitalfields weaver / Stage Struck
325 Robert Macaire
326 Country Squire
327 Athenian Captivo
328 { Barney the Baron / Happy man
329 Der Freischutz

ADVERTISEMENTS.

330 Hush money
331 East Lynne
332 The Robbers
333 The Bottle
334 Kenilworth
335 The mountaineer
336 Simpson and Co.
337 A Roland for an Oliver
338 { Siamese Twins / Turned Head
339 Maid of Croissey
340 Rip Van Winkle
341 Court Fool
342 Uncle Tom's Cabin
343 { Deaf as a Post / Soldier's Courtship
344 Bride of Lammermoor
345 Gwyneth Vaughan
346 Esmeralda
347
348 Town and Country
349 { Middy Ashore / Matteo Falcone
350 Duchess of Malfi
351 Naval Engagements
352 Victorine
353 Spectre Bridegroom
354 Alice Gray
355 { Fish Out of water / Family Jars
356 Rory O'More
357 Zarah
358 { Love in humble Life / 15 Years of Labour Lost
359 Dream of the Future
360 { Mrs. White / Cherry Bounce
361 Elder Brother
362 Robber's wife
363 { Sleeping Draught / Smoked miser
364 Love
365 Fatal Dowry
366 { Bengal Tiger / Kill or cure
367 Paul Clifford
368 Dumb man of Manchester
369 Sergeant's Wife
370 Jonathan Bradford
371 Gilderoy
372 { Diamond cut Diamond / Philippe
373 Legend of Florence
374 David Copperfield
375 Dombey and Son
376 Wardock Kennilson
377 Night and morning
378 Lucretia Borgia
379 Ernest Maltravers
380 { Dancing Barber / Turning the Tables
381 Poor of New York
382 St. Mary's Eve
383 Secrets worth Knowing
384 Carpenter of Rouen
385 Ivanhoe
386 Ladies' club
387 { Hercules / Bears not Beasts
388 Bleak House
389 Colleen Bawn
390 The Shaughraun
391 The Octoroon
392 Sixteen String Jack
393 Barnaby Rudge
394 Cricket on the Hearth
395 Susan Hopley
396 Way to get married
397 Wandering Jew
398 Old Curiosity Shop
399 Under the G
400 Jane Eyre
401 Raffaelle
402 { Hunting a Turtle / Catching a Heiress
403 { Good Night's Rest / Lodgings for Gentlemen
404 The Wren Boys
405 { Swiss cottage / 'Twas I
406 Clari
407 { Sudden Thoughts / How to Pay the Rent
408 Mary, Queen of Scots
409 { The Culprit / Boarding School
410 Lucille
411 { Four Sisters / Nothing to Nurse
412 My Unknown Friend
413 { Young widow / More Blunders than One
414 Woman's Love
415 { A Widow's Victim / Day after the Fair
416 The Jewess
417 { Unfinished Gentleman / Captain is not A-miss
418 Media
419 { The Twins / Uncle's Card
420 Martha Willis
421 { Love's labyrinth / Ladder of love
422 White Boys
423 { Mistress of the mill / Frederick of Prussia
424 Mabel's curse
425 { Perplexing Predicament / A Day in Paris
426 Rye-house Plot
427 Little Jockey
428
429 Dumb Conscript
430 Heart of London
431 Frankenstein
432 Fairy Circle
433 { Sea-bathing at home / Wrong man
434 Farmer's story
435 Lady and the Devil
436 Vanderdecken
437 A poor young man
438 { Under which king? / Tobit's Dog
439 His last legs
440 Life of an Actress
441 White horse of the Peppers
442 Artist's Wife
443 Black Domino
444 Village Outcast
445 Ten Thousand a-Year
446 Beulah Spa
447 Perils of Pippins
448 Barrack Room
449 Richard Plantagenet
450 Red Rover
451 Idiot of Heidelberg
452 The Assignation
453 Groves of Blarney
454 Ask no Questions
455 Ireland as it is
456 Jonathan in England
457 Inkle and Yarico
458 Nervous man
459 Message from the Sea
460 Black Doctor
461 King O'Neil
462 { Forty and Fifty / Tom Noddy's Secret
463 Irish Attorney
464 The Camp
465 St. Patrick's Day
466 Irish Gentleman
467 Village Coquettes
468 Life of a woman
469 Nicholas Nickleby
470 { Is she his wife? / The Lamplighter
471 Fernande
472 Scamps of London
473 Jessie Brown
474 Oscar, the half-blood
475 Mary Ducange
476 Narcisse
477 Little Gerty
478 Obi
479 Austerlitz
480 Grandfather's will
481 Hidden Treasure
482 True as Steel
483 Self-Accusation
484 Crown Prince
485 Yew-Tree Ruins
486 Charles O'Malley
487 { Bandit / The snow helped
488 { Jargonelle / A marriage noose
489 { Lost Pocket-book / Twenty and Forty
490 { All's Fair in Love / Woman will be a woman
491 { Captain's Ghost / Hat-box
492 { No. 157 B / Lovely
493 { Bow Bell(e)s / Mistaken
494 { Locksmith / Portmanteau
495 Ruth
496 Maid of Mariendorpt
497 The Turf
498 Harlequin honx
499 Sweeney Todd
500 My Poll & Partner Joe
501 The King's wager
502 Tower of London
503 { Monsieur Jacques / Plot and counterplot
504 The Birthday
505 Grandfather Whitehead
506 The Stone Jug
507 Jacob Faithful
508 Jack Ketch
509 Bold Dragoons
510 Remorse
511 Old house at home
512 Jersey Girl
513 Haroun Alraschid
514 Beggar's Petition
515 { Own Blue Bell / Grimalkin
516 Paulina
517 { Affair of honour / The Lancers
518 St. Patrick's Eve
519 Mr. Greenfinch
520 The hall porter
521 Prisoner of War
522 { Matching-making / The Dumb Belle
523 Lucky horse-shoe
524 { My wife's dentist / Railroad Station
525 The Schoolfellow
526 { Woman-Hater / Comfortable Service
527 You can't marry your Grandmother
528 Rochester
529 Golden calf
530 Bride of Ludgate
531 { Twice Killed / A Day well spent
532 Tam O'Shanter
533 Woodstock
534 Jack Brag
535 { New Footman / King's Gardener
536 Woman's Faith
537
538 Joconde
539 The Steward
540 Evil Eye
541 Sam Weller
542 Tekeli
543
544 The Roebuck
545 { Little Adopted / Gentleman in Difficulties
546 Wish-ton wish
547 Nick of the woods
548 Faith and Falsehood
549 Lalla Rookh
550
551 One Fault
552 { Jacket of Blue / Cousin Peter
553 Bubbles of the Day
554 Beau Nash
555 Pauvrette
556 Andy Blake
557 Blanche of Jersey
558 { Doctor Dilworth / Fellow clerk
559 Pascal Bruno
560 Wicklow mountains
561 { The Pic-nic / Railway Hotel
562 Fashionable Arrivals
563 Water-Party
564 { Boots at the Swan / Lucky Stars
565 Walter Tyrrel
566 Izaak Walton
567 Wife's Stratagem
568 { Marcelino / The Daughter
569 Field of Forty Footsteps
570 The wigwam
571 Cramond Brig
572 { Infant Phenomenon / Captain Cuttle
573 Faust
574 Jack in the water
575 Man and wife
576 A House Divided
577 John Smith
578 { Long and Short / Lydia's Lover's lodging
579 I and my double
580 Sons and Systems
581 My old woman
582 Life of an Actor
583 Chancery Suit
584 Besieged heart
585 My wife—what wife?
586 Blanche Heriot
587 Lady of the Lake
588 Bill Jones
589 Americans Abroad
590 { Pleasant dreams / Advice Gratis
591 The Wedding Gown
592 Dice of death
593 The Bottle Imp
594 Lost and won
595 Marriage
596 The Three Secrets
597 Frederick the Great
598 A libertine's lesson
599 Jacques Strop
600 The Charming Polly
601 Life's a lottery
602 { Antony and Cleopatra / The Party wall
603 A cure for love
604 Gissipus
605 Helen Oakleigh
606 { Blue-Faced Baboon / Ourang-Outang
607 The White Milliner
608 Perouron
609 The Greek Boy
610 Robespierre
611 The Red Farm
612 Miser's daughter
613 { Wanted, a Brigand / Claude Duval
614 Camille
615 The Pride of Birth
616 Mothers and daughters
617 Belford castle
618 { Duchess of —— / Punch out of town
619 Thomas A'Beckett
620 Mazeppa
621 Temptation
622 Mary Melvin
623 A Night in the Bastille
624 { Rinks, the Bagman / Dobson and Co.
625 The Blind Bargain
626 { Jane, the Licensed Victualler's daughter
627 { Bamboozling / The Sergeant's Wedding
628 The Game of Love
629 Old Maids
630 Gustavus the Third
631 The Weathercock
632 Turpin's Ride to York

ADVERTISEMENTS.

633 Doves in a Cage
634 Ocean of Life
635 Nina Sforza
636 { Bardell v. Pickwick / Two Swindlers
637 Ambrose Gwynett
638 Hazard of the Die
639 Peer and the Peasant
640 One Hundred Pound Note
641 Factory Boy
642 Merchant and his Clerks
643 { Living Statues / My Sister Kate
644 Cavalier
645 Lottery of Life
646 False and Constant
647 Who'll Lend me a Wife
648 'Twould Puzzle a Conjuror
649 Devil's in It
650 Love's Sacrifice
651 { Painter of Ghent / 102
652 Man for the Ladies
653 You Know What
654 Gipsy King
655 Court and City
656 Gertrude's Cherries
657 Legerdemain
658 English Etiquette
659 My Wife's Mother
660 { Humpbacked Lover / Patter v. Clatter
661 { Truth / Ringdoves
662 { Dowager / Why did you Die?
663 Love of a Prince
664 Fanchon, the Cricket
665 Secretary
666 Bringing Home the Bride
667 Charles the First
668 Moonshine
669 { Angeline / Divorce
670 Brian Boroihme
671 Noyades
672 Inez de Castro
673 Love, Law, and Physic
674 Heiress of Bruges
675 Climbing Boy
676 { Married Rake / Conquering Game
677 Haunted Inn
678 Comfortable Lodgings
679 Two Friends
680 French Spy
681 Provost of Bruges
682 Lone Hut
683 { Peter Smink / Mrs. Smith
684 Handy Andy
685 Michael Erle
686 Old Parr
687 Tarnation Strange
688 Royal Oak
689 Rose of Arragon
690 Halvei, the Unknown
691 John of Procida
692 { Serenading / Middle Temple
693 Promise of Marriage
694 Chain of Gold
695 Beggar's Daughter
696 Battle of Waterloo
697 Phantom
698 Gil Blas
699 { My Wife's Out / Borrowing a Husband
700 Arajoun
701 Forced Marriage
702 Valsha
703 { Behind the Scenes / HB
704 Linda, the Pearl of Savoy
705 Lost Ship

706 Roll of the Drum
707 Ambassador's Lady
708 Spring and Autumn
709 Close Siege
710 Louison
711 Our Village
712 Tempter
713 Love's Frailties
714 Surgeon of Paris
715 Lord Darnley
716 School for Grown Children
717 Riches
718 Devil in London
719 { M.P. for the Rotten Borough / Grey Doublet
720 Leola Colomba
721 London by Night
722 Christmas Carol
723 London Banker
724 Master Humphrey's Clock
725 { Omnibus / Mayor of Rochester
726 Game of Life
727 Deserted Village
728 Old and Young Stager
729 Follies of Fashion
730 Romance and Reality
731 Last Shilling
732 Tom Bowling
733 Love Extempore
734 Devil on Two Sticks
735 Maiden's Fame
736 { How's your Uncle / Mistaken Story
737 In the Wrong Box
738 Martin Churzlewit
739 Lilian, the Show Girl
740 { Man about Town / My Friend the Captain
741 Signal
742 Whitefriars
743 Young King
744 Queen's Champion
745 Cæsar, the Watch-Dog
746 Ondine
747 Comrades and Friends
748 { Personation / Antony and Cleopatra / Married and Settled
749 Mary Stuart
750 { Petticoat Government / 'Tis She
751 Corsair's Revenge
752 Corsican Brothers
753 Blind Boy
754 Ben, the Boatswain
755 Rich and Poor
756 Dumb Guide of the Tyrol
757 { British Legion / Rifle Brigade
758 Love Laughs at Locksmiths
759 Sempstress
760 Nelson
761 Daughter of the Regiment
762 Momentous Question
763 { Review / Sylvester Daggerwood
764 Love and Loyalty
765 Delusion
766 Quid pro Quo
767 Charcoal Burner
768 { Gemini / Lying in Ordinary
769 Rose of Ettrick Vale
770 { Valet de Sham / My Valet and I
771 Dream of Fate
772 { Maidens Beware / Pink of Politeness
773 Ancestress
774 { Is he Jealous? / Three and the Deuce
775 Loss of the Royal George

776 { Day at an Inn / Gentleman in Black
777 Double Gallant
778 { Aldgate Pump / Bump of Benevolence
779 Philosophers of Berlin
780 Tale of Two Cities
781 Ambition
782 { Queer Subject / Deeds of Dreadful Note
783 Youthful Queen
784 { Teddy the Tiler / Born to Good Luck
785 Hard Times
786 Spare Bed
787 Wager
788 Fair Rosamond
789 Notoriety
790 Factory Strike
791 Point of Honour
792 Shakspeare's Early Days
793 Folly as it Flies
794 St. Clair of the Isles
795 Mutiny at the Nore
796 John Overy
797 Two Fishermen of Lynn
798 Mysterious Stranger
799 Education
800 Don Cæsar de Bazan
801 Single Life
802 Married Life
803 Dream at Sea
804 { Our Mary Anne / Mischief-Making
805 Agnes de Vere
806 Wreck Ashore
807 Boyne Water
808 { Shocking Events / Dead Shot
809 Lesson for Ladies
810 Love and Murder
811 Rural Felicity
812 Presumptive Evidence
813 Poor Jack
814 Abelard and Heloise
815 Duchess de la Vaubaliere
816 { John Jones / Christening
817 Isabel
818 May Queen
819 Chimes
820 Home Again
821 Henriette, the Forsaken
822 { Irish Lion / Brother Tom
823 Rake and his Pupil
824 Pet of the Petticoats
825 Marianne, the Child of Charity
826 Toodles
827 Green Bushes
828 Don Juan
829 Last Days of Pompeii
830 Luke the Labourer
831 Death Fetch
832 Maid of Athens
833 Beggar Boy of Brussels
834 Scholar
835 Forgery
836 Uncle John
837 Ellen Wareham
838 Open House
839 Second Thoughts fat-Law
840 Nicholas Flam, Attorney-
841 Snakes in the Grass
842 { 23, John Street, Adelphi / Thimble Rig
843 Sheriff of the Country
844 Happiest Day of My Life
845 Weak Points
846 Good Husbands make Good Wives
847 Duchess de la Valliere
848 { Damon and Pythias / Two Queens

849 Dame de St. Tropez
850 Husband at Sight
851 Time Works Wonders
852 { Kiss in the Dark / Match in the Dark
853 How to Grow Rich
854 King of the Alps
855 Our New Governess
856 Victorine
857 Mysterious Family
858 Hasty Conclusions
859 Leah the Forsaken
860 Ladies' Battle
861 Jacopo the Bravo
862 Peter Bell the Waggoner
863 The Bear-Hunters
864 Josephine, the Child of the Regiment
865 { Popping the Question / Snapping Turtles
866 { Maid with the Milking Pail / Billy Taylor
867 Theodore the Brigand
868 Cabdriver
869 Follies of a Night
870 Secret Service
871 Charles the Twelfth
872 Doom of Marana
873 { Welsh Girl / Pleasant Neighbour
874 Spanish Curate
875 Vampire
876 Brigand
877 Child of the Wreck
878 { Faint Heart Never Won Fair Lady / Peculiar Position
879 Merchant's Wedding
880 Woman Never Vext
881 { Trip to Kissengen / Garrick Fever
882 Who's your Friend?
883 Court Favour
884 Regent
885 Ransom
886 Paris and London
887 { Hasty Conclusion / Handsome Husband
888 Two Figaros
889 { Cabinet Question / Printer's Devil
890 Grist to the Mill
891 Green-Eyed Monster
892 Reputation
893 { Captain of the Watch / Promotion
894 Returned "Killed"
895 { Loan of a Lover / Somebody Else
896 All in the Dark
897 { My Daughter, Sir! / My Great Aunt
898 { Court Beauties / Peter and Paul
899 { Jenkinses / My Friend, the Governor
900 Bonnie Prince Charlie
901 Memoirs of the Devil
902 Ruy Blas
903 The Delinquent
904 Chain of Guilt
905 Life as It Is
906 { One Hour / Matrimony
907 Smuggler Boy
908 Exchange no Robbery
909 Freemason
910 Simon Lee
911 Dramatist
912 { All at Coventry / Poor Soldier
913 Dream Spectre
914 { He Lies like Truth / State Secrets

Each Play is Illustrated, and printed from the Original Work of the Author, without Abridgment. To the Theatrical Profession, Amateurs, and others, this edition is invaluable, as full stage directions costumes, &c., are given. All the back numbers are in print, and can be purchased separately, one penny each, or per post, 1½d.   London: JOHN DICKS, 313, Strand. All Booksellers.

ADVERTISEMENTS.

DICKS' PIANOFORTE TUTOR.

This book is full music size, and contains instructions and exercises, full of simplicity and melody, which will not weary the student in their study, thus rendering the work the best Pianoforte Guide ever issued. It contains as much matter as those tutors for which six times the amount is charged. The work is printed on toned paper of superior quality, in good and large type. Price One Shilling; post free, Twopence extra.

CZERNY'S STUDIES FOR THE PIANOFORTE.

These celebrated Studies in precision and velocity, for which the usual price has been Half-a-Guinea, is now issued at One Shilling; post free, threepence extra. Every student of the Pianoforte ought to possess this companion to the tutor to assist him at obtaining proficiency on the instrument.

DICKS' EDITION OF STANDARD OPERAS (full music size), with Italian, French, or German and English Words. Now ready:—
  DONIZETTI'S "LUCIA DI LAMMERMOOR," with Portrait and Memoir of the Composer. Price 2s. 6d.
  ROSSINI'S "IL BARBIERE," with Portrait and Memoir of the Composer. Price 2s. 6d.
  Elegantly bound in cloth, gilt lettered,

SIMS REEVES' SIX CELEBRATED TENOR SONGS, Music and Words. Price One Shilling. Pilgrim of Love. Bishop.—Death of Nelson. Braham.—Adelaide, Beethoven.—The Thorn. Shield.—The Anchor's Weighed. Braham.—Tell me, Mary, how to Woo Thee. Hodson.

ADELINA PATTI'S SIX FAVOURITE SONGS, Music and Words. Price One Shilling. There be none of Beauty's Daughters. Mendelssohn.—Hark, hark, the Lark. Schubert.—Home, Sweet Home. Bishop.—The Last Rose of Summer. T. Moore.—Where the Bee Sucks. Dr. Arne.—Tell me, my Heart. Bishop.

CHARLES SANTLEY'S SIX POPULAR BARITONE SONGS. Music and Words. Price One Shilling. The Lads of the Village. Dibdin.—The Wanderer. Schubert.—In Childhood My Toys. Lortzing.—Tom Bowling. Dibdin.—Rock'd in the Cradle of the Deep. Knight.—Mad Tom. Purcell.

MUSICAL TREASURES.— Full Music size, price Twopence.

1
2 Auld Robin Gray (Scotch Ballad)
3
4
5 Di Pescatore (Song)
6 To Far-off Mountain (Duet)
7
8 A Woman's Heart (Ballad)
9
10 Above, how Brightly Beams the Morning
11 The Marriage of the Roses (Valse)
12 Norma (Duet)
13 Lo! Heavenly Beauty (Cavatina)
14 In Childhood my Toys (Song)
15 While Beauty Clothes the Fertile Vale
16 The Harp that once through Tara's Halls
17
18 Beethoven's "Andante and Variations"
19
20
21
22 La Petit Fleur
23 Angels ever Bright and Fair
24
25
26 My Mother bids me Bind my Hair (Canzonet)
27
28
29
30
31
32 Hommage au Genie
33 See what Pretty Brooms I've Bought
34
35
36
37
38
39 As it Fell upon a Day (Duet)
40 A Life on the Ocean Wave (Song)
41 Why are you Wandering here I pray? (Ballad)
42 A Maiden's Prayer.

43 Valse Brillante
44 Home, Sweet Home! (Song)
45 Oft in the Stilly Night (Song)
46 Ali's Well (Duet)
47 The "Crown Diamonds" Fantasia
48 Hear me, dear One (Serenade)
49 Youth and Love at the Helm (Barcarolle)
50 Adelaide Beethoven (Song)
51 The Death of Nelson (Song)
52
53
54 The Thorn (Song)
55
56 There be none of Beauty's Daughters (Song)
57
58 I have Plucked the Fairest Flower
59 Bid Me Discourse (Song)
60 Fisher Maiden (Song)
61 Fair Agnes (Barcarolle)
62 How Calm and Bright (Song)
63 Woman's Inconstancy (Song)
64 Echo Duet
65 The Meeting of the Waters (Irish Melody)
66 Lo, Here the Gentle Lark
67 Beethoven's Waltzes (Second Series)
68 Child of Earth with the Golden Hair (Song)
69 Should he Upbraid (Song)
70 Lieder ohne Worte. Nos. 4 and 9
71 Waft her, Angels
72 Movement from Sonata in A
73 What is this Feeling?
74 Romance in F-major
75 With Verdure Clad
76 Derniere Pensee
77 Love in her Eyes sits Playing
78 Andante from Sonata in G
79 Yea, the Lord is Mindful of his Own
80 He shall Feed his Flock like a Shepherd
81 Pastoral Symphony
82 Impromptu in A-Flat
83 The Hunt is Up.
84 I Dreamt that I Dwelt in Marble Halls
85 Slumber Song

London: JOHN DICKS, 313, Strand; and all Booksellers.

ADVERTISEMENTS.

CELEBRATED WORKS.
THE CHEAPEST BOOKS IN THE WORLD.

THE PILGRIM'S PROGRESS. By John Bunyan.
PEOPLE'S EDITION, 2d.; postage, one halfpenny. Complete, from original, without abridgment.

DON JUAN. By Lord Byron.
PEOPLE'S EDITION, 6d.; postage, 1½d. Complete, from original, without abridgment.

THE VICAR OF WAKEFIELD. By Oliver Goldsmith.
PEOPLE'S EDITION, 2d.; postage, one halfpenny. Complete, from original, without abridgment.

THE LADY OF THE LAKE. By Sir Walter Scott.
PEOPLE'S EDITION, 2d.; postage, one halfpenny. Complete, from original, without abridgment.

SIEGE OF CORINTH, PRISONER OF CHILLON, &c. By Lord Byron.
PEOPLE'S EDITION, 1d.; postage, one halfpenny. Complete, from original, without abridgment.

LALLA ROOKH. By Thomas Moore.
PEOPLE'S EDITION, 3d.; postage, one halfpenny. Complete, from original, without abridgment.

THE CORSAIR. By Lord Byron.
PEOPLE'S EDITION, 1d.; postage, one halfpenny. Complete, from original, without abridgment.

MARMION. By Sir Walter Scott.
PEOPLE'S EDITION, 2d.; postage, one halfpenny. Complete, from original, without abridgment.

CHILDE HAROLD'S PILGRIMAGE. By Lord Byron.
PEOPLE'S EDITION, 2d.; postage, one halfpenny. Complete, from original, without abridgment.

SINDBAD THE SAILOR. From "The Arabian Nights."
PEOPLE'S EDITION, 1d.; postage, one halfpenny. Complete, without abridgment.

PAUL AND VIRGINIA. By Bernardin de Saint-Pierre.
PEOPLE'S EDITION, 2d.; postage, one halfpenny. Translated from original, without abridgment.

RASSELAS, PRINCE OF ABISSINIA. By Dr. Samuel Johnson.
PEOPLE'S EDITION, 2d.; postage, one penny. Complete, from original, without abridgment.

ALADDIN; or, the WONDERFUL LAMP. From "The Arabian Nights."
PEOPLE'S EDITION, 1d.; postage, one halfpenny. Complete, without abridgment.

THE CASTLE OF OTRANTO. By Horace Walpole.
PEOPLE'S EDITION, 2d.; postage, one halfpenny. Complete, without abridgment.

THE THREE CALENDERS. From "The Arabian Nights."
PEOPLE'S EDITION, 1d.; postage, one halfpenny. Complete, without abridgment.

ALI BABA AND THE FORTY ROBBERS. From "The Arabian Nights."
PEOPLE'S EDITION, 1d.; postage one halfpenny. Complete, without abridgment.

NOUREDDIN AND THE FAIR PERSIAN. From "The Arabian Nights."
PEOPLE'S EDITION, 1d.; postage, one halfpenny. Complete, without abridgment.

ABOULHASSEN ALI EBN BECAR. From "The Arabian Nights."
PEOPLE'S EDITION, 1d.; postage, one halfpenny. Complete, without abridgment.

THE VAMPYRE. By Lord Byron.
PEOPLE'S EDITION, 1d.; postage, one halfpenny. Complete, without abridgment.

THE ACTOR'S HAND-BOOK. By The Old Stager.
PEOPLE'S EDITION, 3d.; postage one halfpenny. Complete, without abridgment.

TWO DROVERS, & AUNT MARGARET'S MIRROR. By Sir Walter Scott.
PEOPLE'S EDITION, 1d.; postage, one halfpenny. Complete, without abridgment.

GANEM, THE SLAVE OF LOVE. From "The Arabian Nights."
PEOPLE'S EDITION, 1d.; postage, one halfpenny. Complete, without abridgment.

THE SURGEON'S DAUGHTER. By Sir Walter Scott.
PEOPLE'S EDITION, 2d.; postage, one halfpenny. Complete, without abridgment.

ALMORAN AND HAMET. By Dr. Hawkesworth.
PEOPLE'S EDITION, 2d.; postage, one halfpenny. Complete, from original, without abridgment.

ELIZABETH; OR, THE EXILES OF SIBERIA. By Madame Cottin.
PEOPLE'S EDITION, 2d.; postage, one halfpenny. Complete, from original, without abridgment.

STORY OF THE LITTLE HUNCHBACK. From "The Arabian Nights."
PEOPLE'S EDITION, 2d.; postage, one halfpenny. Complete, without abridgment.

ZADIG; OR, THE BOOK OF FATE. By Voltaire.
PEOPLE'S EDITION, 2d.; postage, one halfpenny. Complete, from original, without abridgment.

SOLYMAN AND ALMENA. By Dr. John Langhorne.
PEOPLE'S EDITION, 1d.; postage, one halfpenny. Complete, from original, without abridgment.

London: JOHN DICKS, 313, Strand. All Booksellers.

ADVERTISEMENTS.

Now Ready, Price 3d.

THE ACTOR'S HAND-BOOK,
AND
GUIDE TO THE STAGE FOR AMATEURS.

HOW TO STUDY.
HOW TO READ.
HOW TO DECLAIM.
HOW TO IMPROVE THE VOICE.
HOW TO MEMORIZE.
HOW TO MAKE UP THE FIGURE.
HOW TO MAKE UP THE FACE.
HOW TO TREAD THE STAGE.

HOW TO MANAGE THE HANDS.
HOW TO EXPRESS THE VARIOUS PASSIONS AND EMOTIONS.
HOW TO DO BYE-PLAY.
HOW TO COMPORT YOURSELF AS A LADY OR GENTLEMAN.
HOW TO OBTAIN AN ENGAGEMENT.

BY THE OLD STAGER.

London: JOHN DICKS, 313, Strand. All Booksellers.

Now Publishing, One Penny, Weekly,

DICKS' STANDARD PLAYS
AND
FREE ACTING DRAMA.

For the Representation of which there is no Legal Charge

Comprising the Works of the most Celebrated Dramatists. Each Play is printed without Abridgment, from the Original work of the Author, and handsomely Illustrated.

To the Theatrical Profession, Amateurs, and others, this edition will prove invaluable as full stage directions, costumes, &c., are given.

Remit penny stamp to the Publisher, and receive a list of over Five Hundred Plays already published.

London: JOHN DICKS, 313, Strand. All Booksellers.

DICKS' STANDARD PLAYS.

esd Twins
ied Head
f Crolsey
m Winkle
Fool
Tom's Cabin
l as a Post
ier's Courtship
of Lammermoor
aeth Vaughan
alda

and Country
ly Ashore
teo Falcone
ss of Malfi
Engagements
ine
e Bridegroom
Gray
h Out of water
nily Jars
O'More

re in humble Life
Years of the Future
n of the Future
a. White
erry Bounce
Brother
er's Wife
eping Draught
oked miser

Dowry
igal Tiger
l or cure
Clifford
) man of Manchester
aut's Wife
han Bradford
roy
mond cut Diamond
lippe
id of Florence
l Copperfield
iey and Son
ock Kenniloon
; and morning
itia Borgia
t Maltravers
icing Barber
ning the Tables
of New York
ary's Eve
s worth Knowing
nter of Rouen
oe
s' club
rcules
rs not Beasts
House
n Bawn
haughraun
ectoroon
n String Jack
by Rudge
on the Hearth
iey
rried
op
ight

ing a Turtle
ating a Heiress
Night's Rest
ings for Gentlemen
en Boys
s cottage
as 1

len Thoughts
to Pay the Rent
Queen of Scots
Culprit
ding School

411 Four Sisters
    Nothing to Nurse
412 My Unknown Friend
413 Young widow
    More Blunders than One
414 Woman's Love
415 A Widow's Victim
    Day after the Fair
416 The Jewess
417 Unfinished Gentleman
    Captain is not A-miss
418 Media
419 The Twins
    Uncle's Card
420 Martha Willis
421 Love's labyrinth
    Ladder of love
422 White Boys
423 Mistress of the mill
    Frederick of Prussia
424 Mabel's curse
425 Perplexing Predicament
    A Day in Paris
426 Rye-house Plot
427 Little Jockey
428
429 Dumb Conscript
430 Heart of London
431 Frankenstein
432 Fairy Circle
433 Sea-bathing at home
    Wrong man
434 Farmer's Story
435 Lady and the Devil
436 Vanderdecken
437 A poor young man
438 Under which king?
    Tobit's Dog
439 His last legs
440 Life of an Actress
441 White horse of the Peppers
442 Artist's Wife
443 Black Domino
444 Village Outcast
445 Ten Thousand a-Year
446 Beulah Spa
447 Perils of Pippins
448 Barrack Room
449 Richard Plantagenet
450 Red Rover
451 Idiot of Heidelberg
452 The Assignation
453 Groves of Blarney
454 Ask no Questions
455 Ireland as it is
456 Jonathan in England
457 Inkle and Yarico
458 Nervous man
459 Message from the Sea
460 Black Doctor
461 King O'Neil
462 Forty and Fifty
    Tom Noddy's Secret
463 Irish Attorney
464 The Camp
465 St. Patrick's Day
466 Strange Gentleman
467 Village Coquettes
468 Life of a woman
469 Nicholas Nickleby
470 Is she his wife?
    The Lamplighter
471 Fernande
472 Scamps of London
473 Jessie Brown
474 Oscar, the half-blood
475 May Ducange
476 Narcisse
477 Little Gerty
478 Obi
479 Austerlitz
480 Grandfather's will
481 Hidden Treasure
482 True as Steel
483 Self-Accusation
484 Crown Prince
485 Yew-Tree Ruins
486 Charles O'Malley

487 Bandit
    The snow helped
488 Jargonello
    A marriage noose
489 Lost Pocket-book
    Twenty and Forty
490 All's Fair in Love
    Woman will be a woman
491 Captain's Ghost
    Hat-box
492 No. 157 B
    Lovely
493 Bow Bell(e)s
    Mistaken
494 Locksmith
    Portmanteau
495 Ruth
496 Maid of Mariendorpt
497 The Turf
498 Harlequin hoax
499 Sweeney Todd
500 My Poll & Partner Joe
501 The King's wager
502 Tower of London
503 Monsieur Jacques
    Plot and counterplot
504 The Birthday
505 Grandfather Whitehead
506 The Stone Jug
507 Jacob Faithful
508 Jack Ketch
509 Bold Dragoon
510 Rer
511 Ol . .ouse at home
512 Jersey Girl
513 Haroun Alraschid
514 Beggar's Petition
515 Own Blue Bell
    Grimalkin
516 Paulina
517 Affair of honour
    The Lancers
518 St. Patrick's Eve
519 Mr. Greenfinch
520 The hall porter
521 Prisoner of War
522 Matching-making
    The Dumb Belle
523 Lucky horse-shoe
524 My wife's dentist
    Railroad Station
525 The Schoolfellow
526 Woman-Hater
    Comfortable Service
527 You can't marry your Grandmother
528 Rochester
529 Golden calf
530 Bride of Ludgate
531 Twice Killed
    A Day well spent
532 Tam O'Shanter
533 Woodstock
534 Jack Brag
535 New Footman
    King's Gardener
536 Woman's Faith
537
538 Joconde
539 The Steward
540 Evil Eye
541 Sam Weller
542 Tekeli
543
544 The Roebuck
545 Little Adopted
    Gentleman in Difficulties
546 Wish-ton wish
547 Nick of the woods
548 Faith and Falsehood
549 Lalla Rookh
550
551 One Fault
552 Jacket of Blue
    Cousin Peter
553 Bubbles of the Day
554 Beau Nash
555 Pauvrette
556 Andy Blake

557 Blanche of Jersey
558 Doctor Dilworth
    Fellow clerk
559 Pascal Bruno
560 Wicklow mountains
561 The Pic-nic
    Railway Hotel
562 Fashionable Arrivals
563 Water-Party
564 Boots at the Swan
    Lucky Stars
565 Walter Tyrrel
566 Izaak Walton
567 Wife's Stratagem
568 Marceline
    The Daughter
569 Field of Forty Footsteps
570 The wigwam
571 Cramond Brig
572 Infant Phenomenon
    Captain Cuttle
573 Faust
574 Jack in the water
575 Man and wife
576 A House Divided
577 John Smith
578 Long and Short
    Lydia's Lover's lodgings
579 I and my double
580 Sons and Systems
581 My old woman
582 Life of an Actor
583 Chancery Suit
584 Bequeathed heart
585 My wife—what wife?
586 Blanche Heriot
587 Lady of the Lake
588 Bill Jones
589 Americans Abroad
590 Pleasant dreams
    Advice Gratis
591 The Wedding Gown
592 Dice of death
593 The Bottle Imp
594 Lost and won
595 Marriage
596 The Three Secrets
597 Frederick the Great
598 A libertine's lesson
599 Jacques Strop
600 The Charming Polly
601 Life's a lottery
602 Antony and Cleopatra
    The Party wall
603 A cure for love
604 Gissipus
605 Helen Oakleigh
606 Blue-Faced Baboon
    Ourang-Outang
607 The White Milliner
608 Percourou
609 The Greek Boy
610 Robespierre
611 The Red Farm
612 Miser's daughter
613 Wanted, a Brigand
    Claude Duval
614 Camille
615 The Pride of Birth
616 Mothers and daughters
617 Belford castle
618 Duchess of ——
    Punch out of town
619 Thomas A'Beckett
620 Mazeppa
621 Temptation
622 Mary Melvin
623 A Night in the Bastille
624 Blinks, the Bagman
    Dobson and Co.
625 The Blind Bargain
626 June, the Licensed Victualler's daughter
627 Bamboozling
    The Sergeant's Wedding
628 The Game of Love

Play is Illustrated, and printed from the Original Work of the Author.
he Theatrical Profession, Amateurs, and others, this edition is invaluable, as full stage
as, costumes, &c., are given.

back numbers are in print, and can be purchased separately. One penny each, or per post, 1½d.

CPSIA information can be obtained
at www.ICGtesting.com
Printed in the USA
BVOW06s0415261017
498617BV00018BA/368/P